About my coloring book!

When my son Craig suggested I do a coloring book, I remembered my Aunt Adelle and all the coloring books she gave me as a child. Well, since I am drawing and creating every day anyway, I thought I would give it a try. So here is my first adult coloring book that is suitable for all ages. It is a great way to relax and to relieve stress;
to be creative and inspired.
Have fun coloring and sharing your
creativity with others.
Enjoy!
Steve Stein

Acknowledgements

Thank you Aunt Adelle for giving me my first coloring book when I was three years old and for inspiring me to be an artist.

Thank you to my family for all their help and support through the years.

Many thanks to my wife Joan, my children, Craig, Lisa, Mark, Jamie, and my grandchildren, Cole, Julia, Hudson and Ryder

In memory of my son in law
Kevin Feinbloom

A portion of the proceeds from the sale of this book will be donated to the *F.I.T.S.* Foundation; a foundation in support of children with cancer.

All illustrations are hand drawn and digitally scanned.

Blank pages intended to help with bleed through.

For more information please visit:
stevesteingallery.com
fansinthestands.org
or kindly email
stevesteingallery@gmail.com
Design: Craig Stein

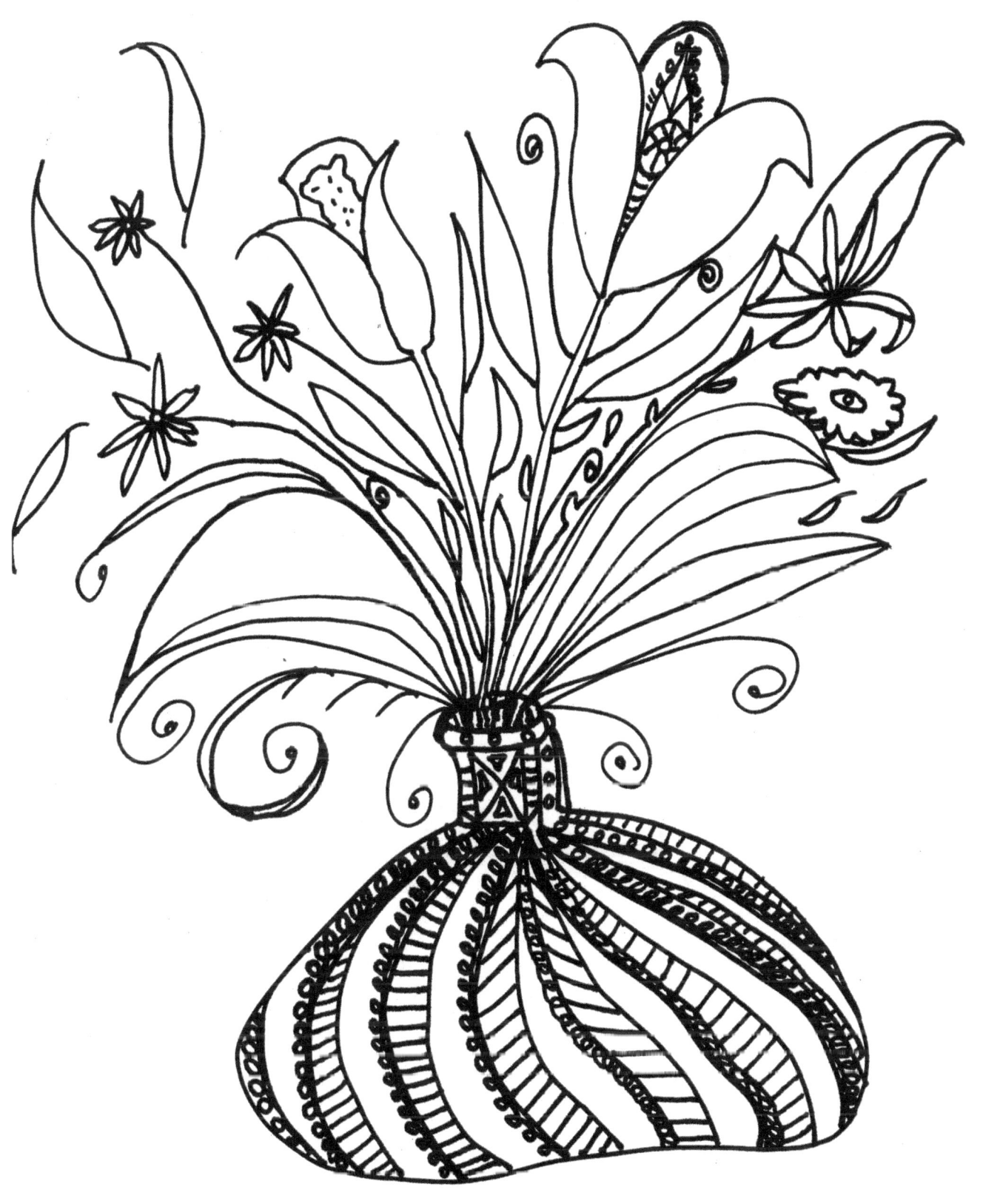

ENCHANTED FLORALS

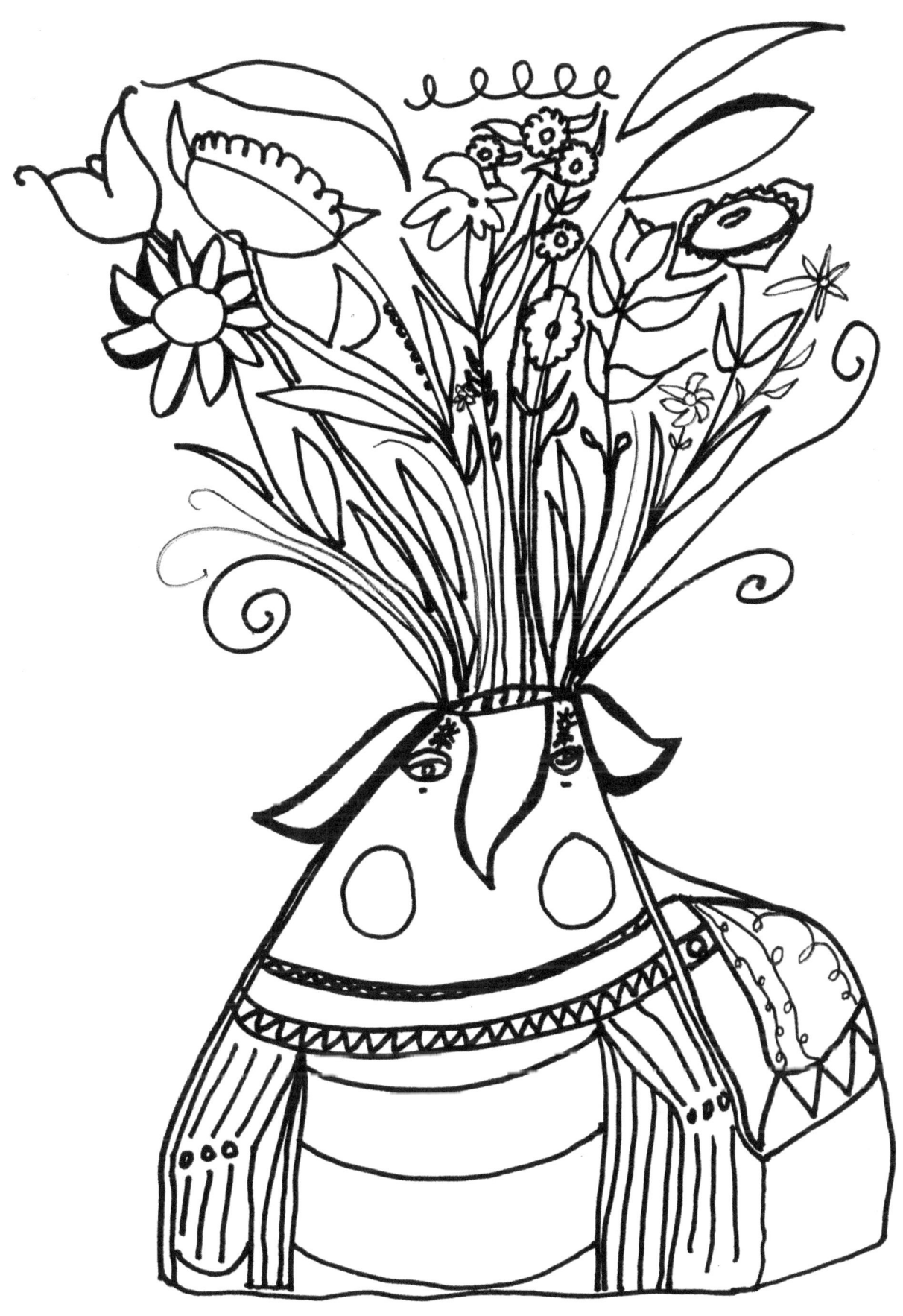

ENCHANTED FLORALS

ENCHANTED FLORIDA

ENCHANTED FLORIDA

ENCHANTED FLORALS

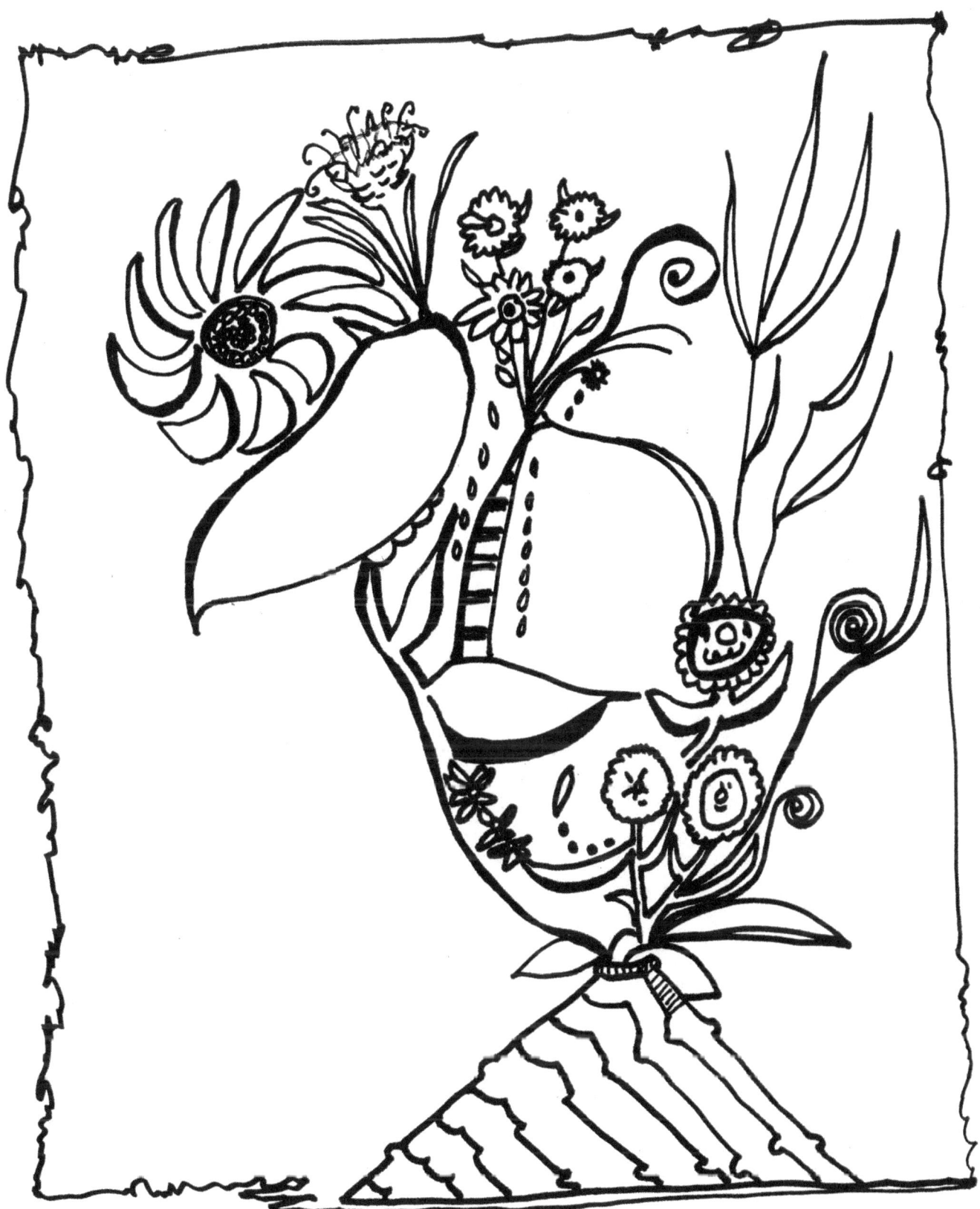

ENCHANTED FLORALS

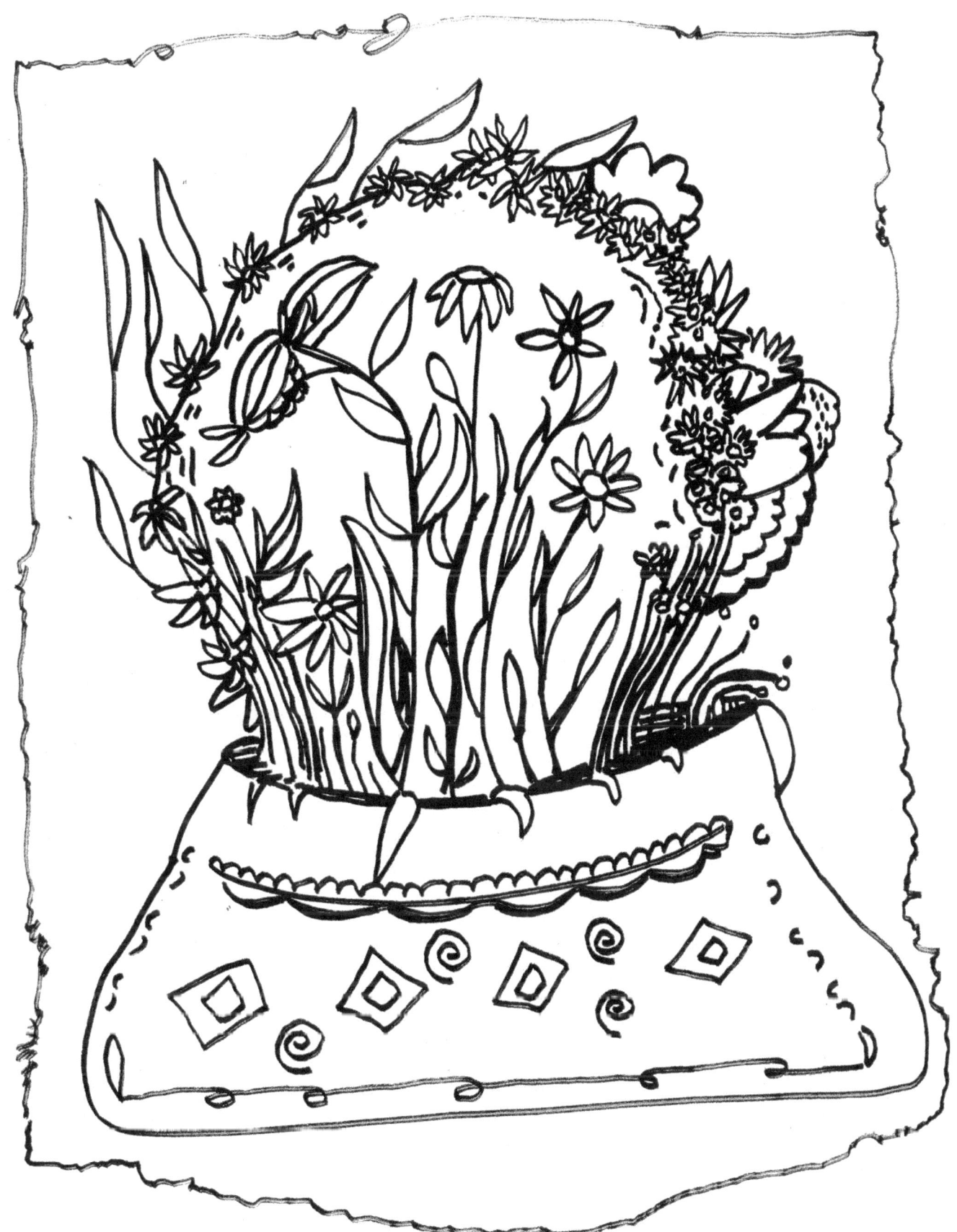

ENCHANTED FLORALS

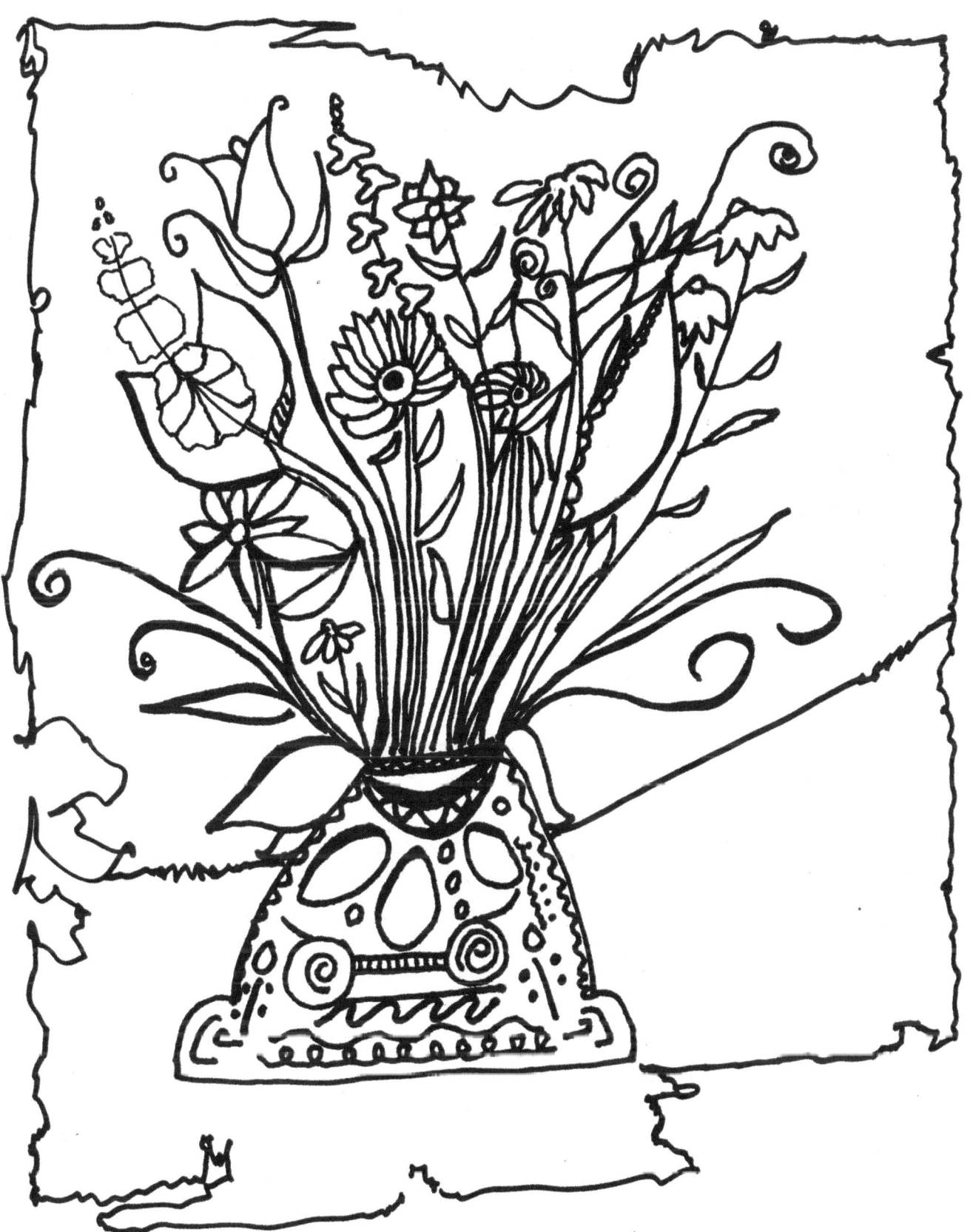

ENCHANTED FLORALS

ENCHANTED FLORALS

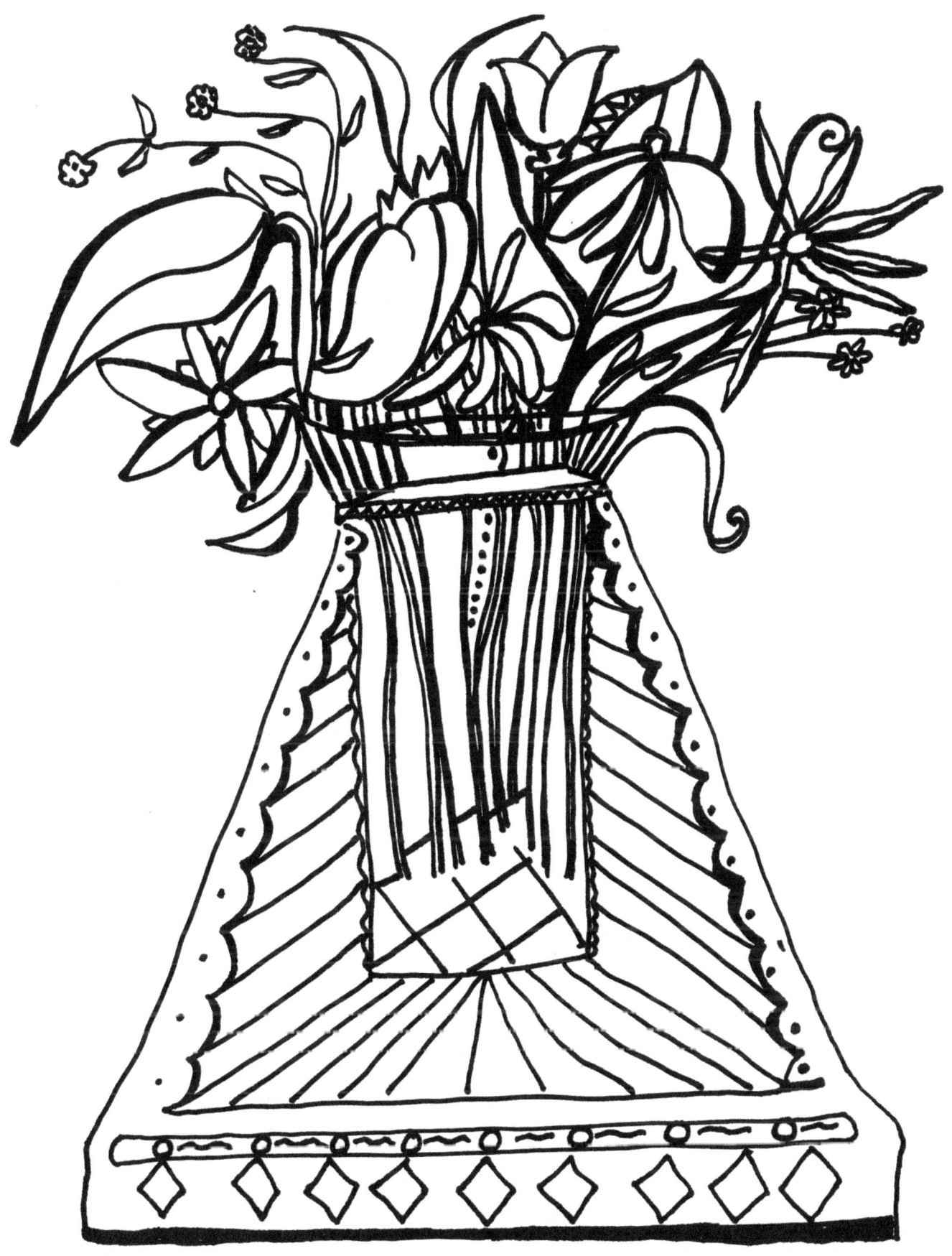

ENCHANTED FLORALS

ENCHANTED FLORALS

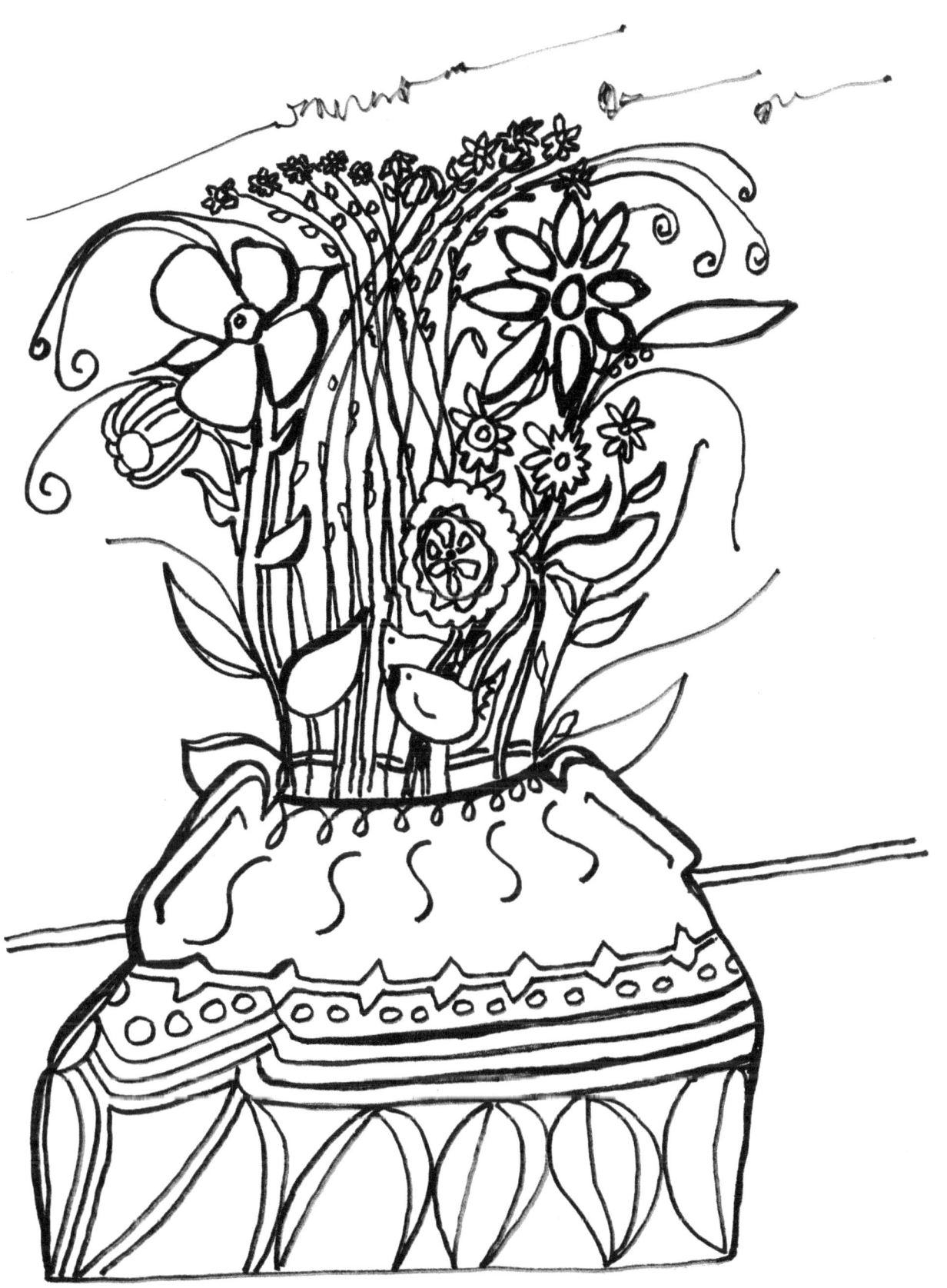

ENCHANTED FLORALS

ENCHANTED FLORALS

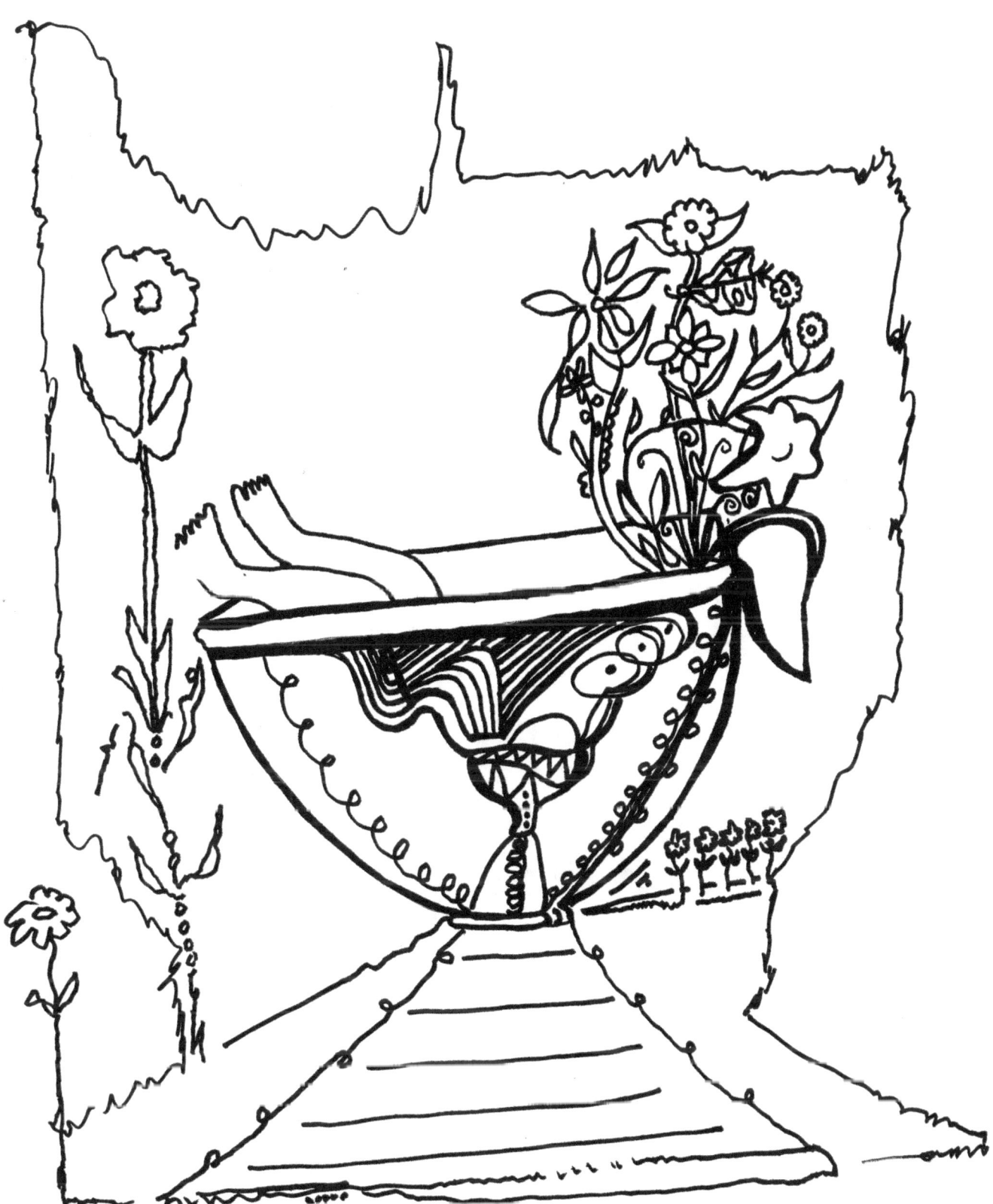

ENCHANTED FLORALS

ENCHANTED FLORALS

ENCHANTED FLORALS

ENCHANTED FLORALS

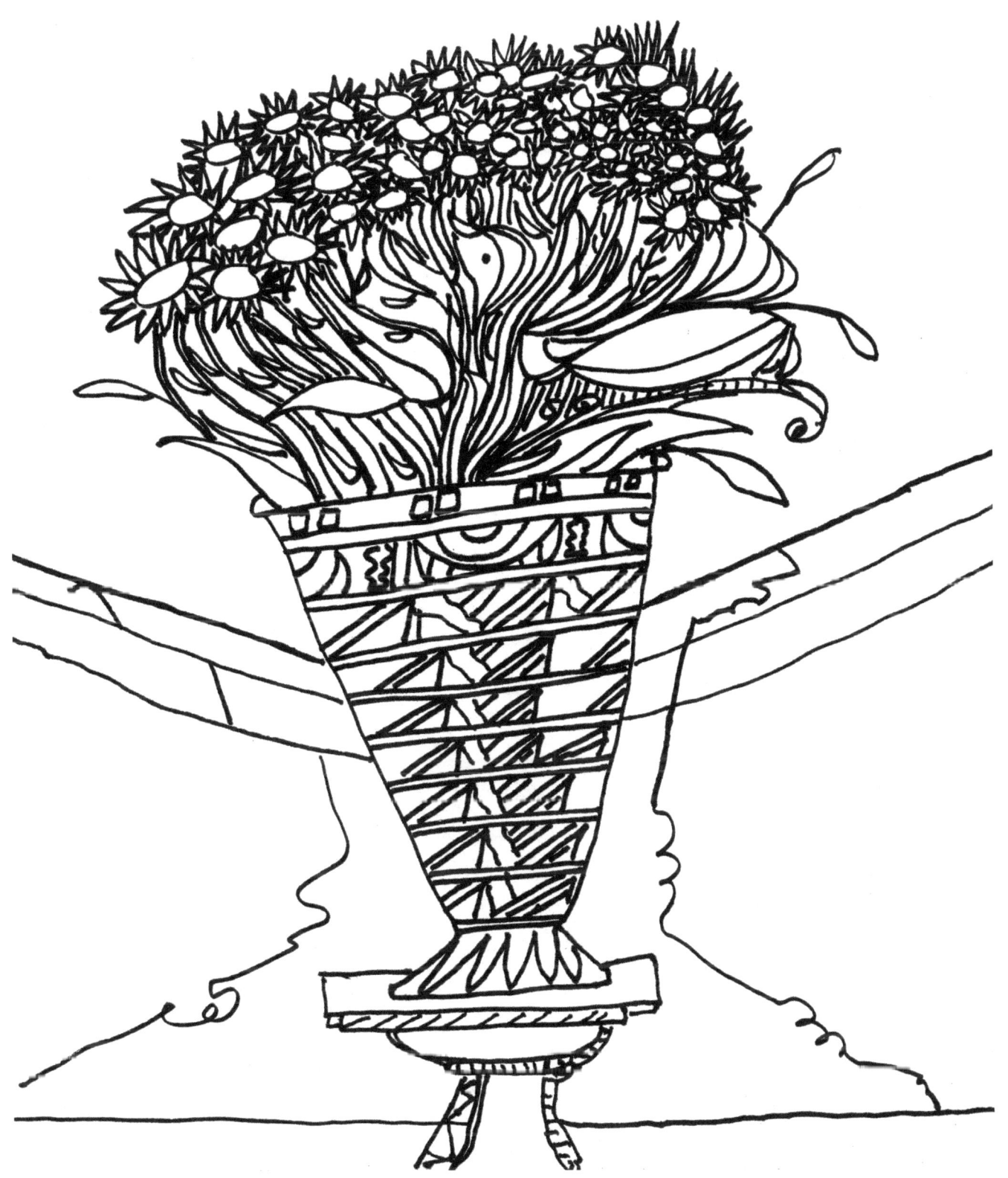

ENCHANTED FLORALS

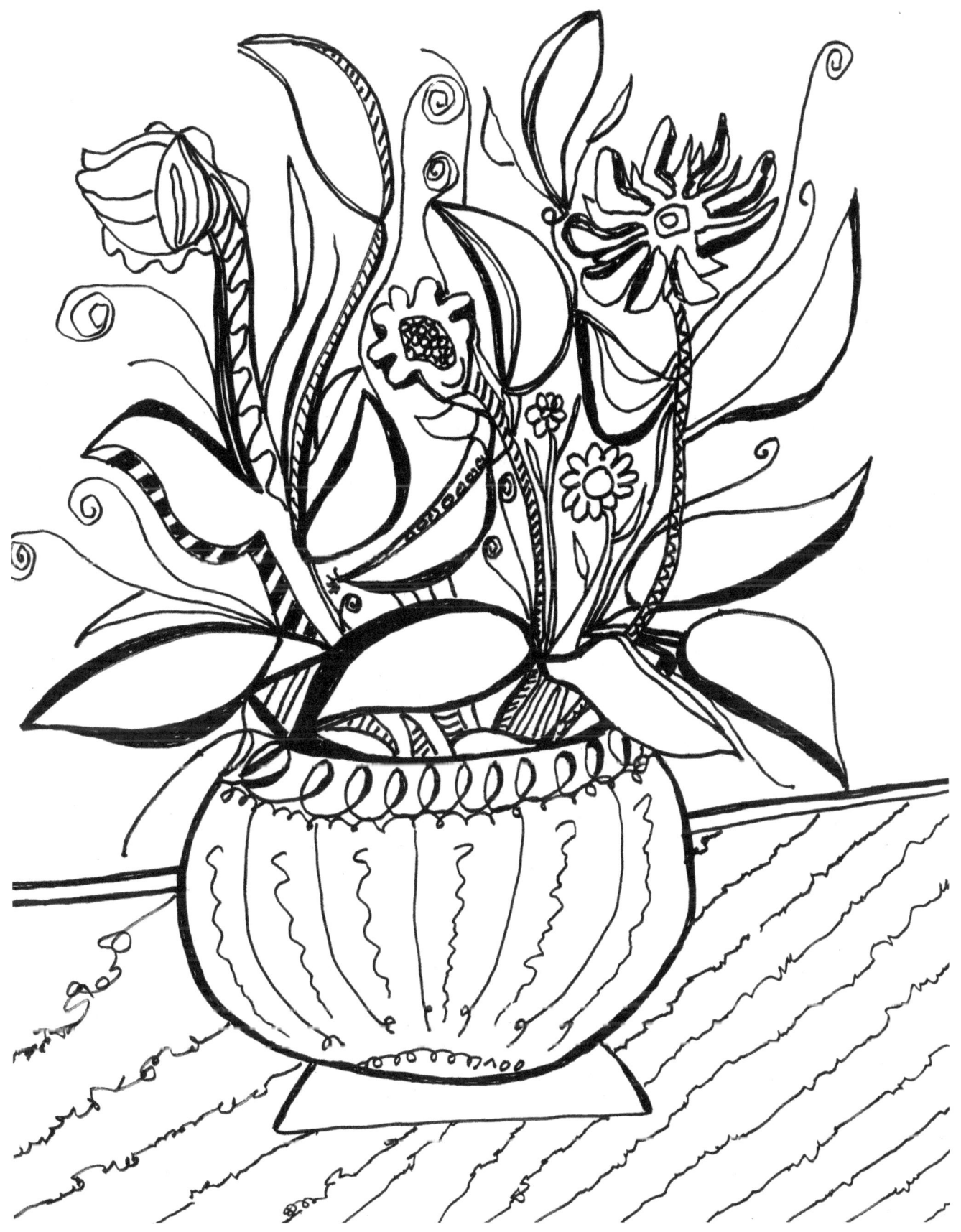

ENCHANTED FLORALS

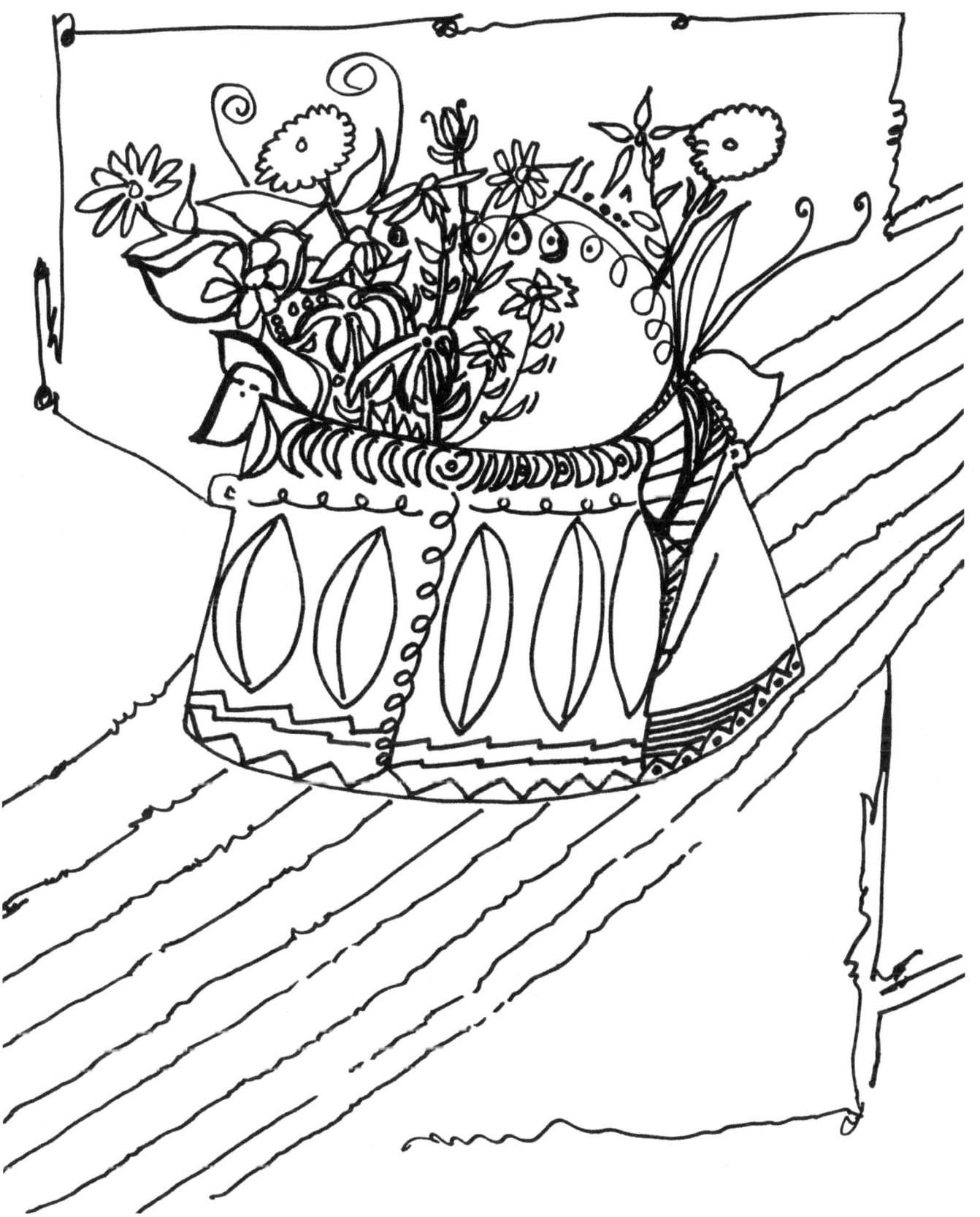

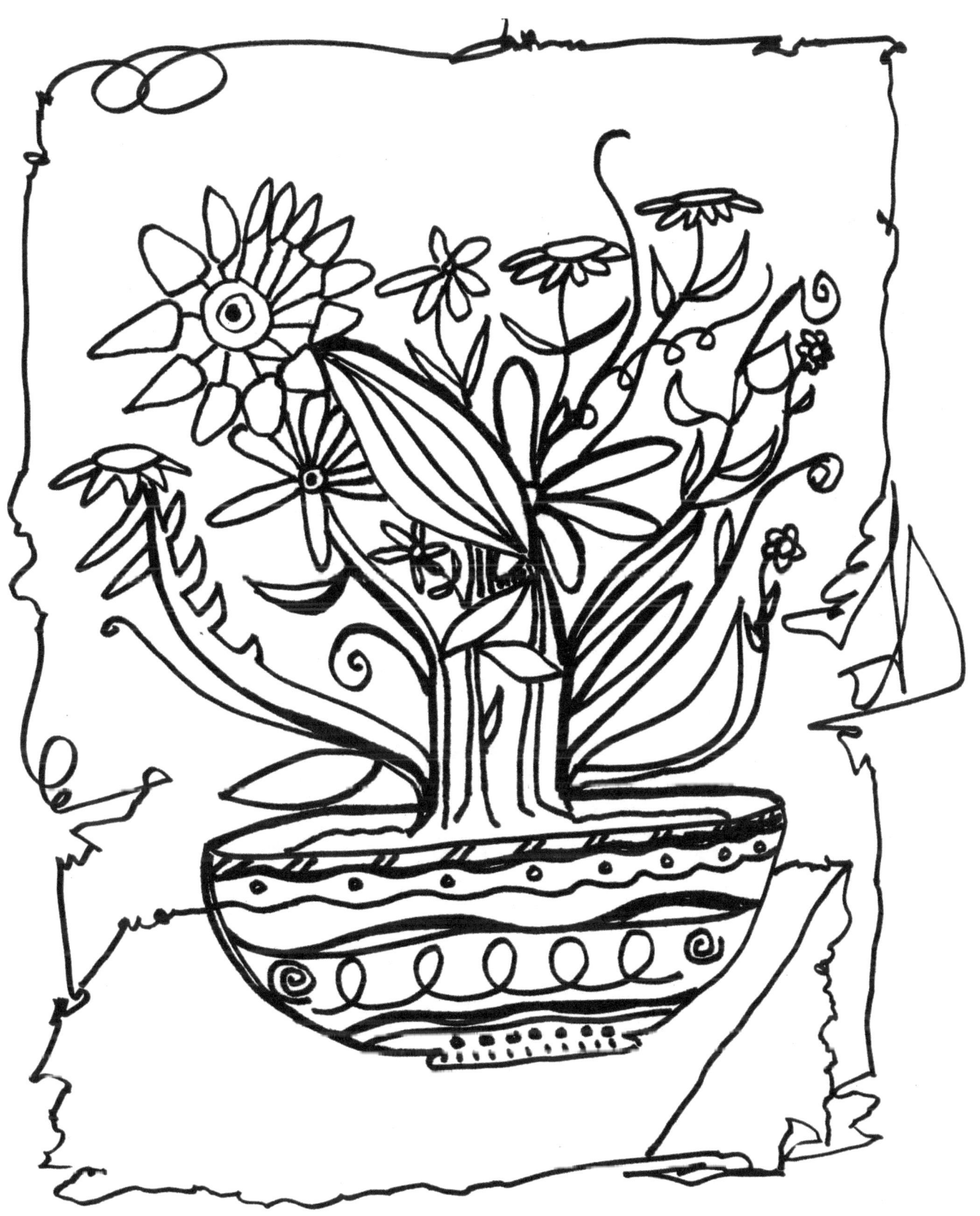

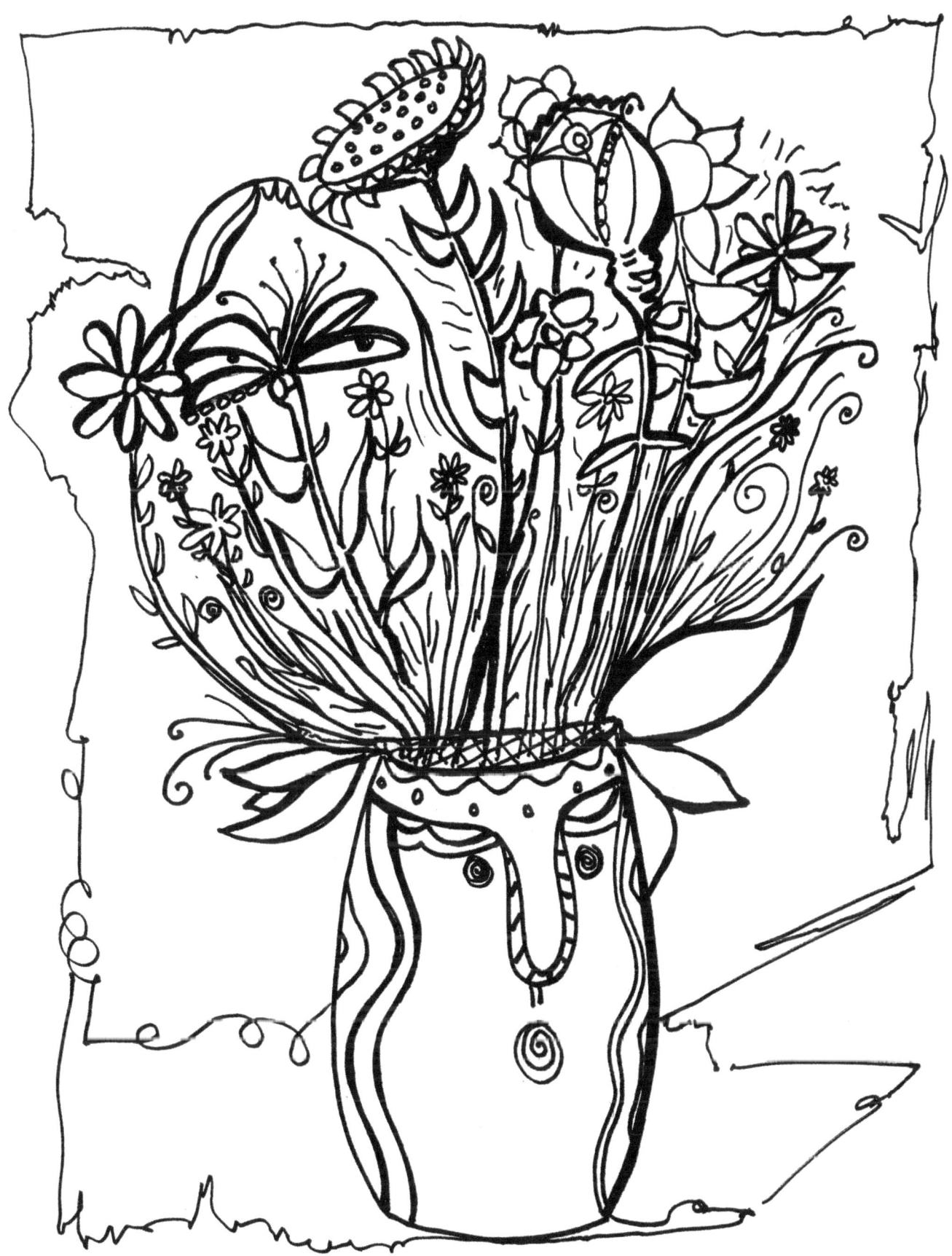

ENCHANTED FLORALS

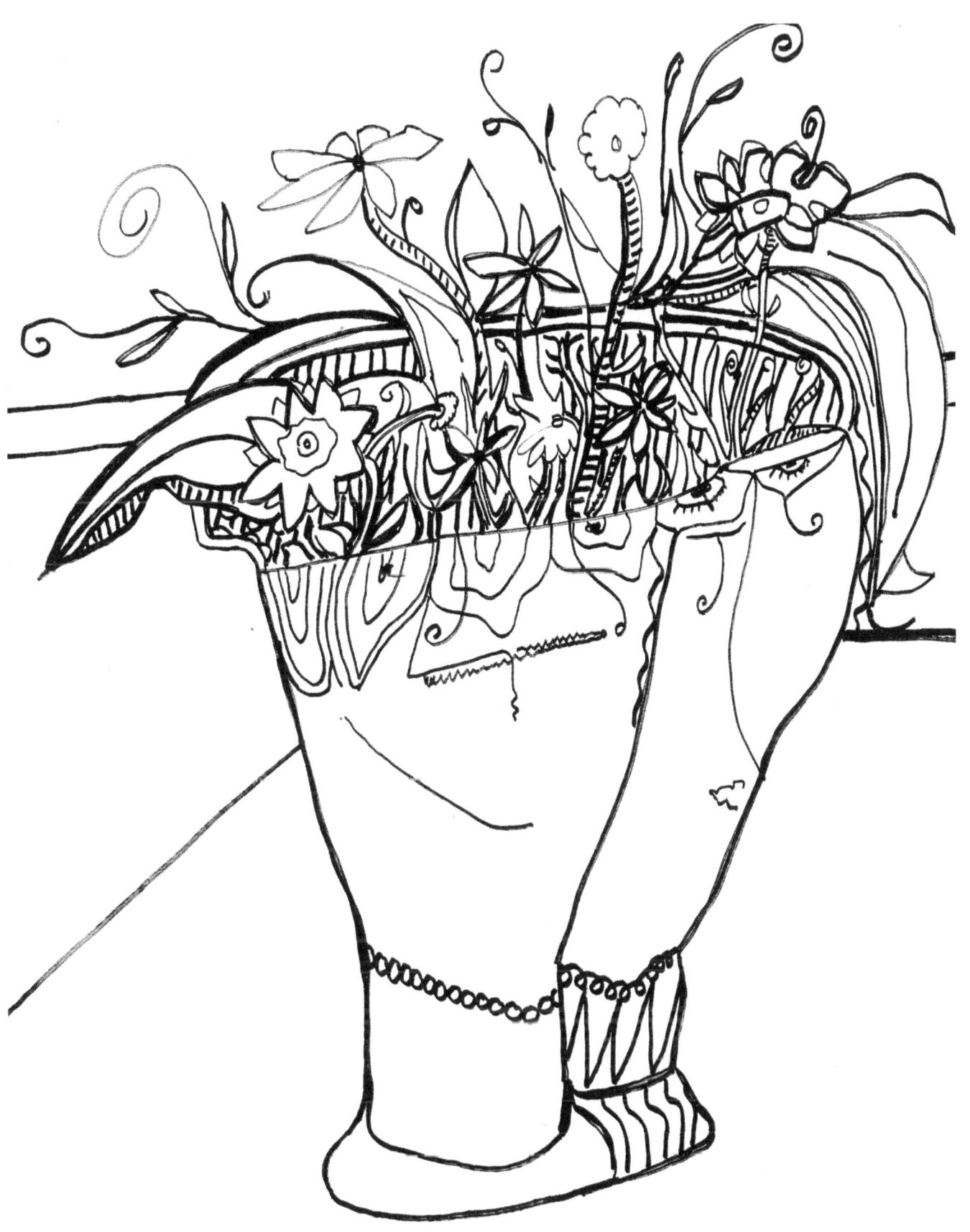

ENCHANTED FLORALS

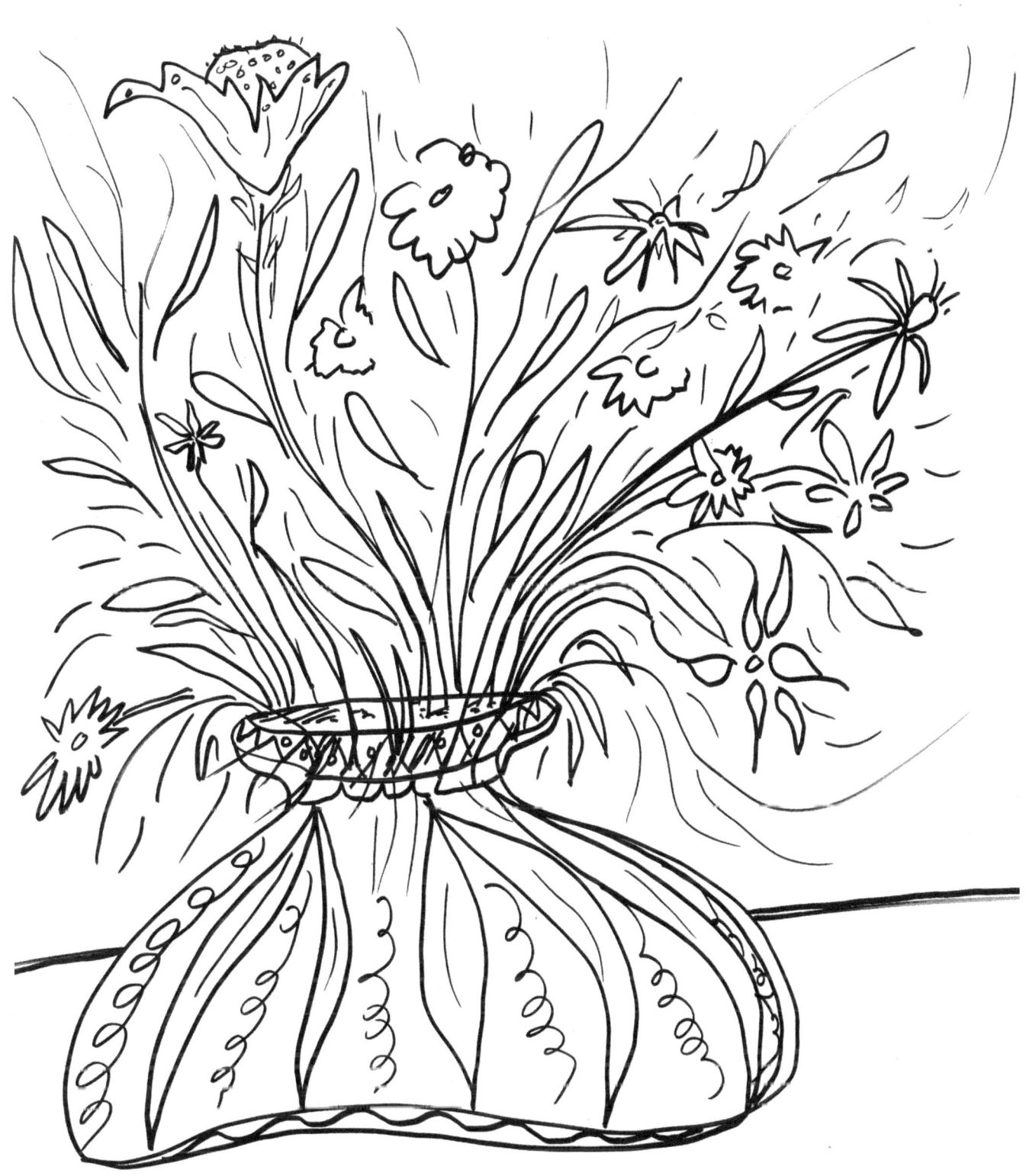

ENCHANTED FLORALS

ENCHANTED FLORALS

ENCHANTED FLORALS

ENCHANTED FLORALS

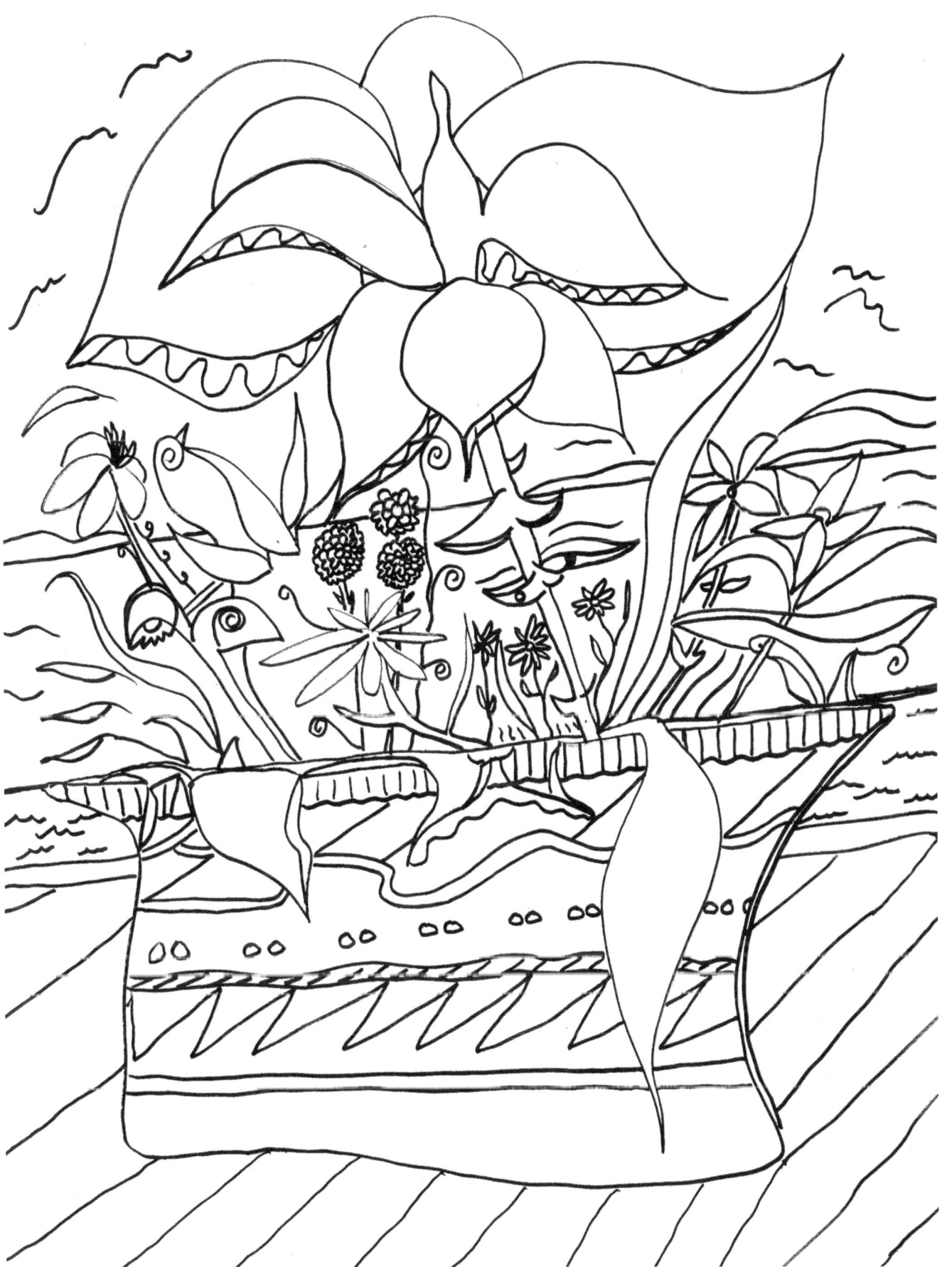

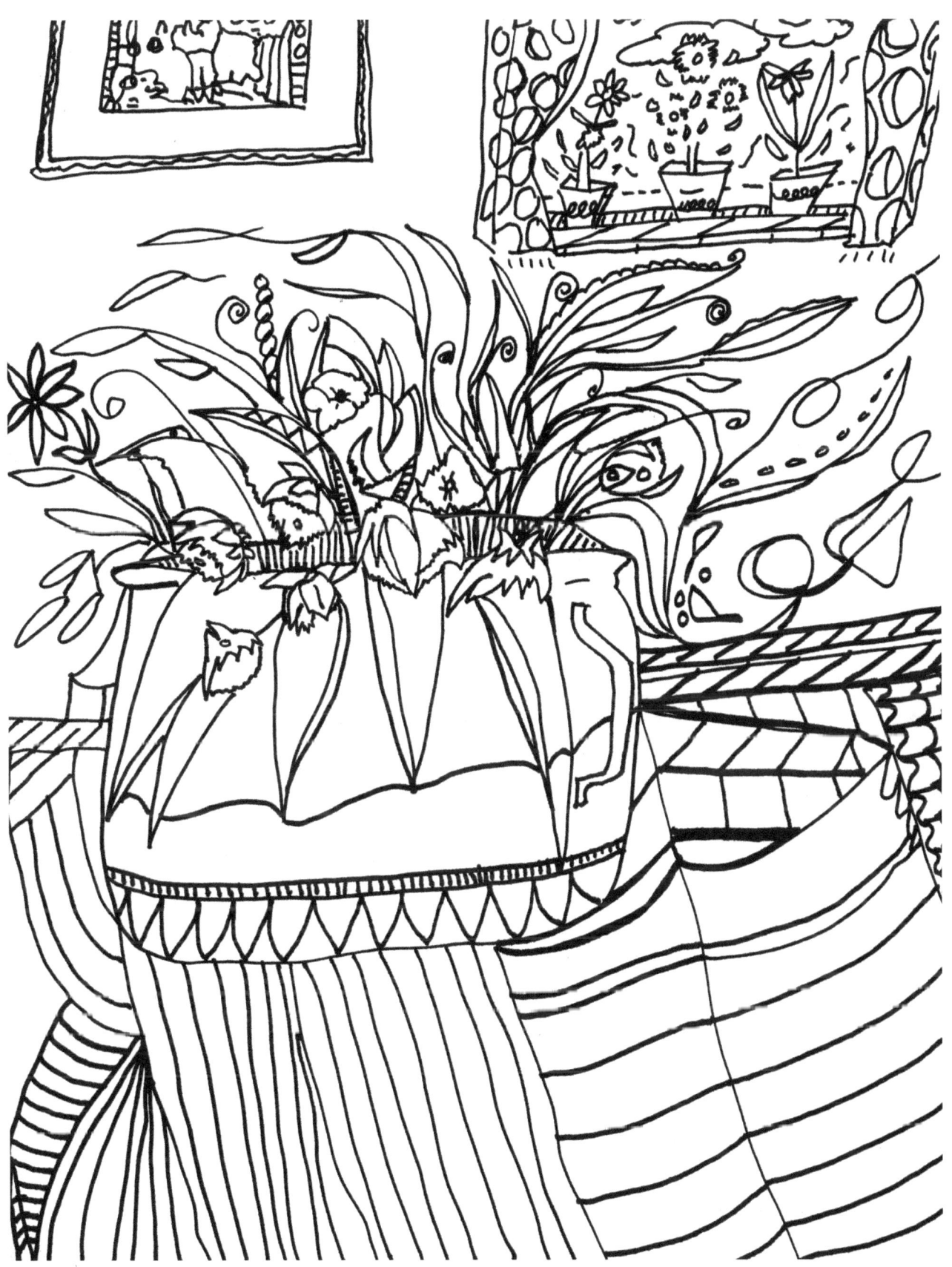

ENCHANTED FLORALS

ENCHANTED FLORALS

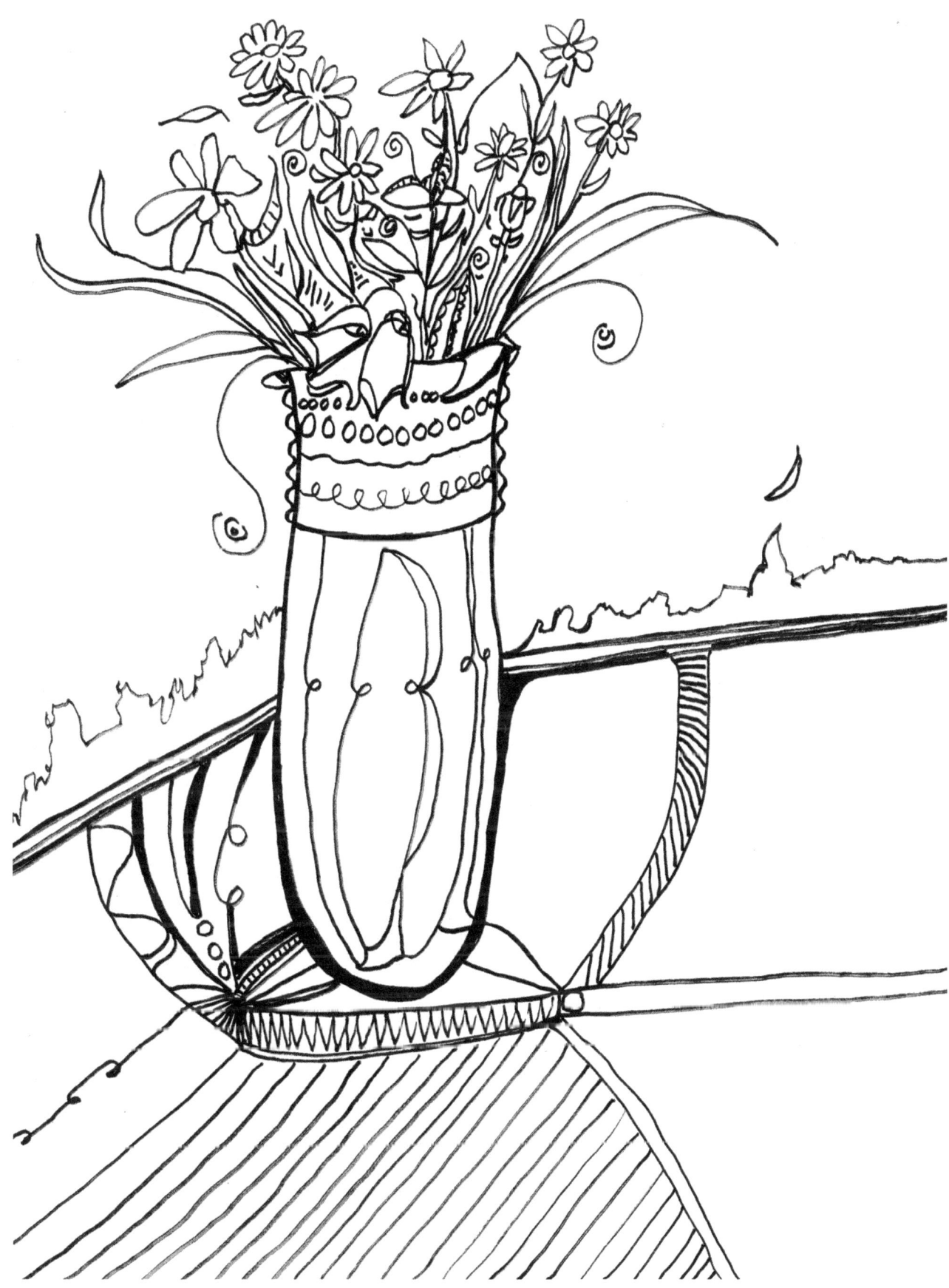

ENCHANTED FLORALS

ENCHANTED FLORALS

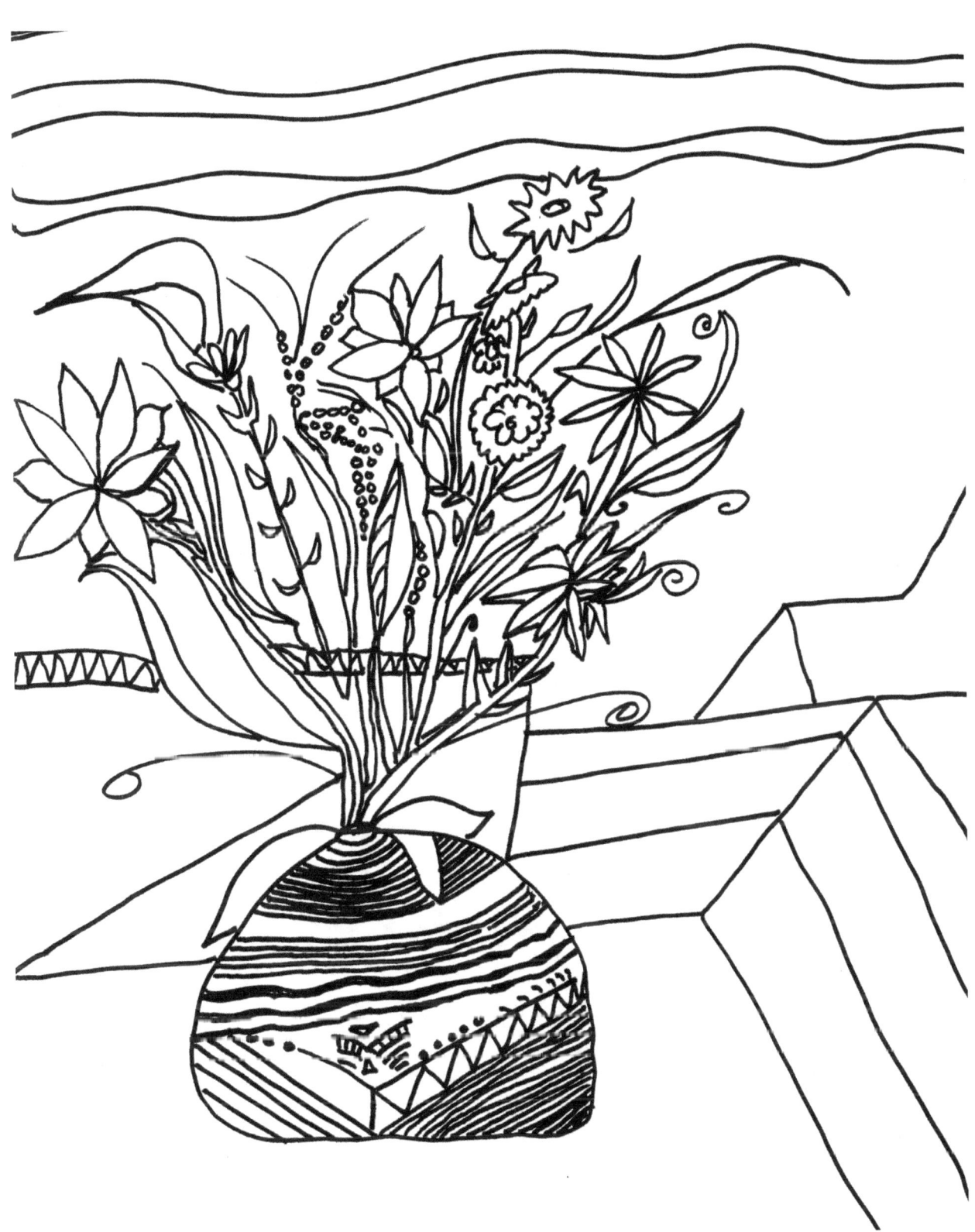

ENCHANTED FLORALS

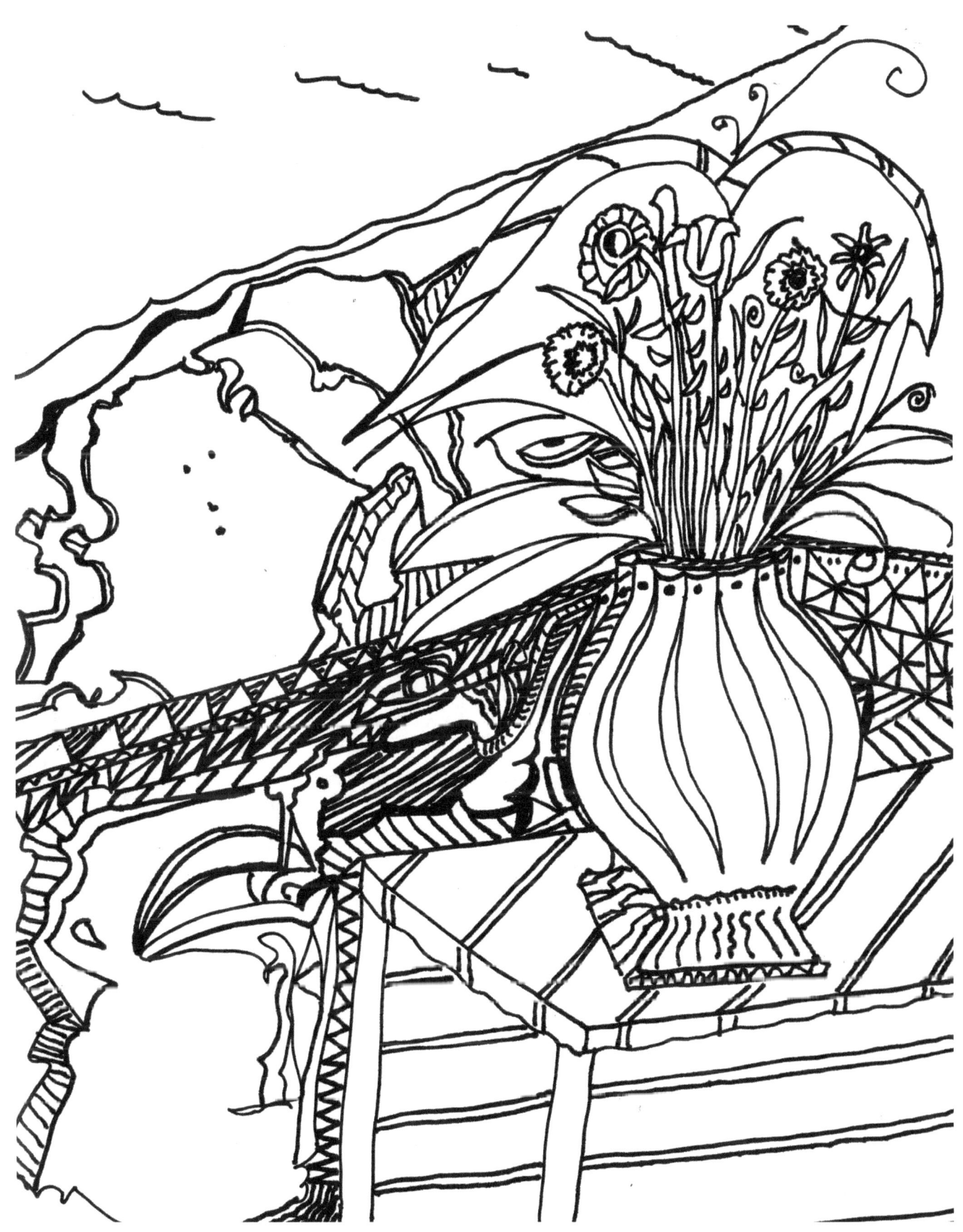

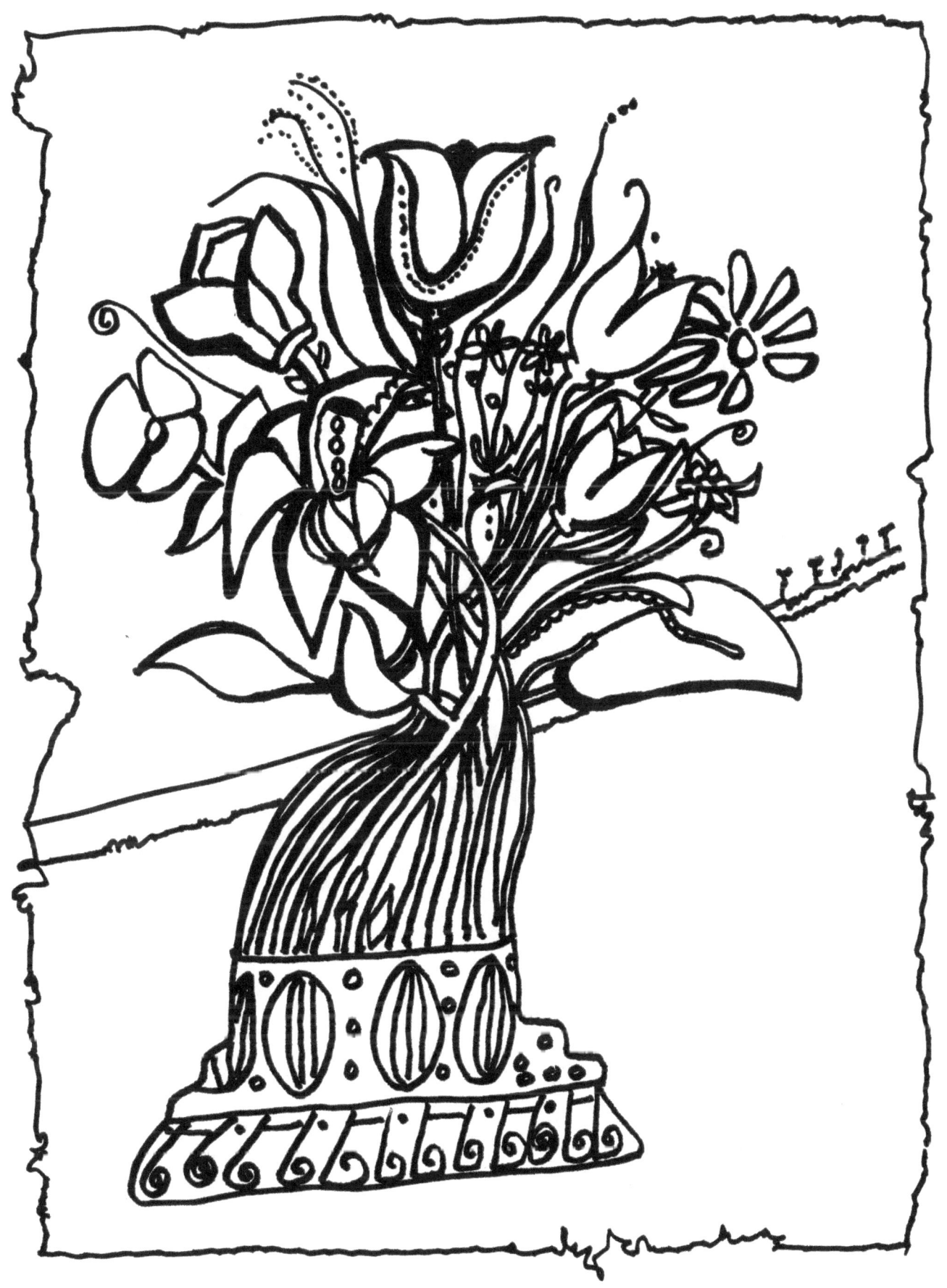

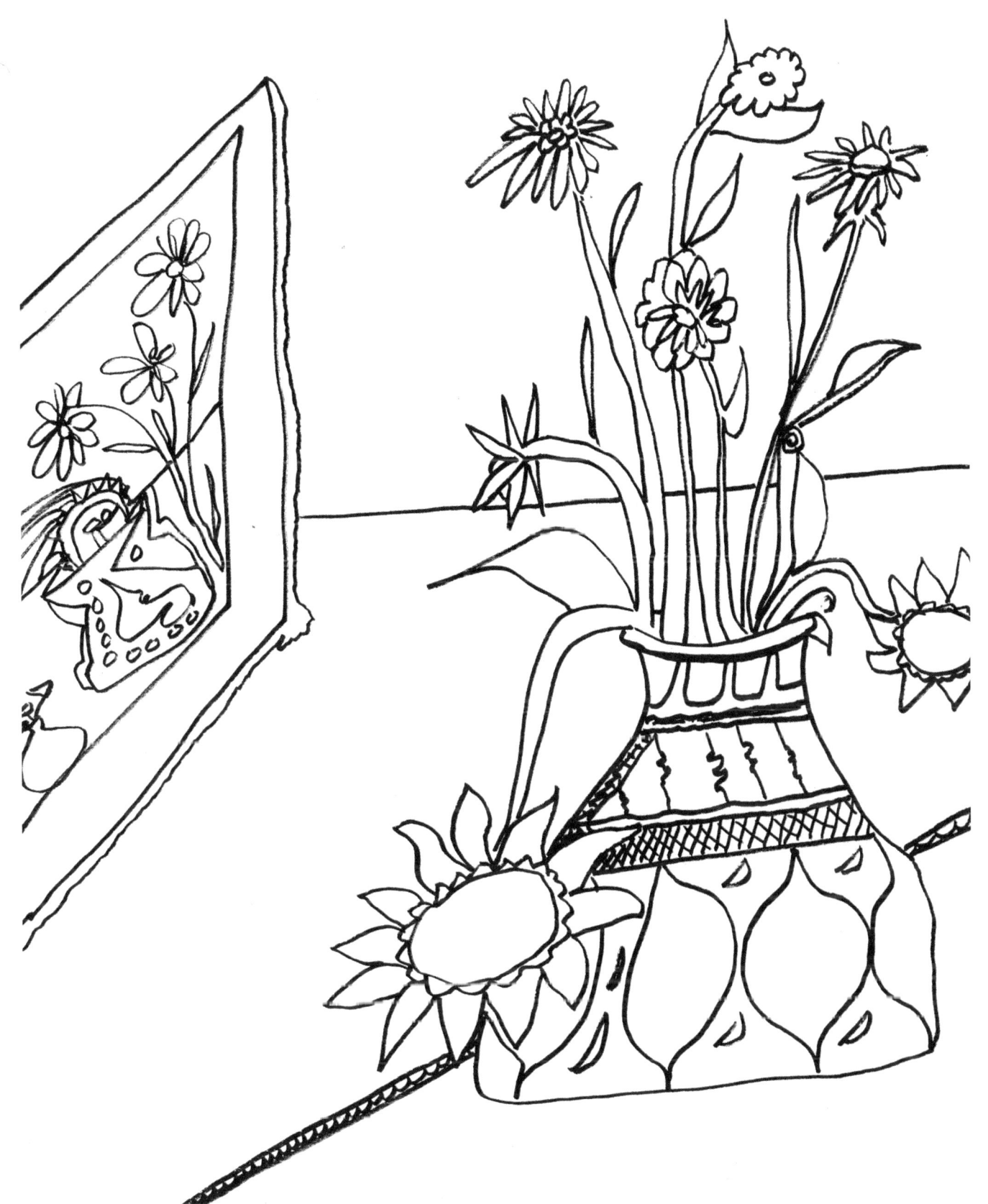

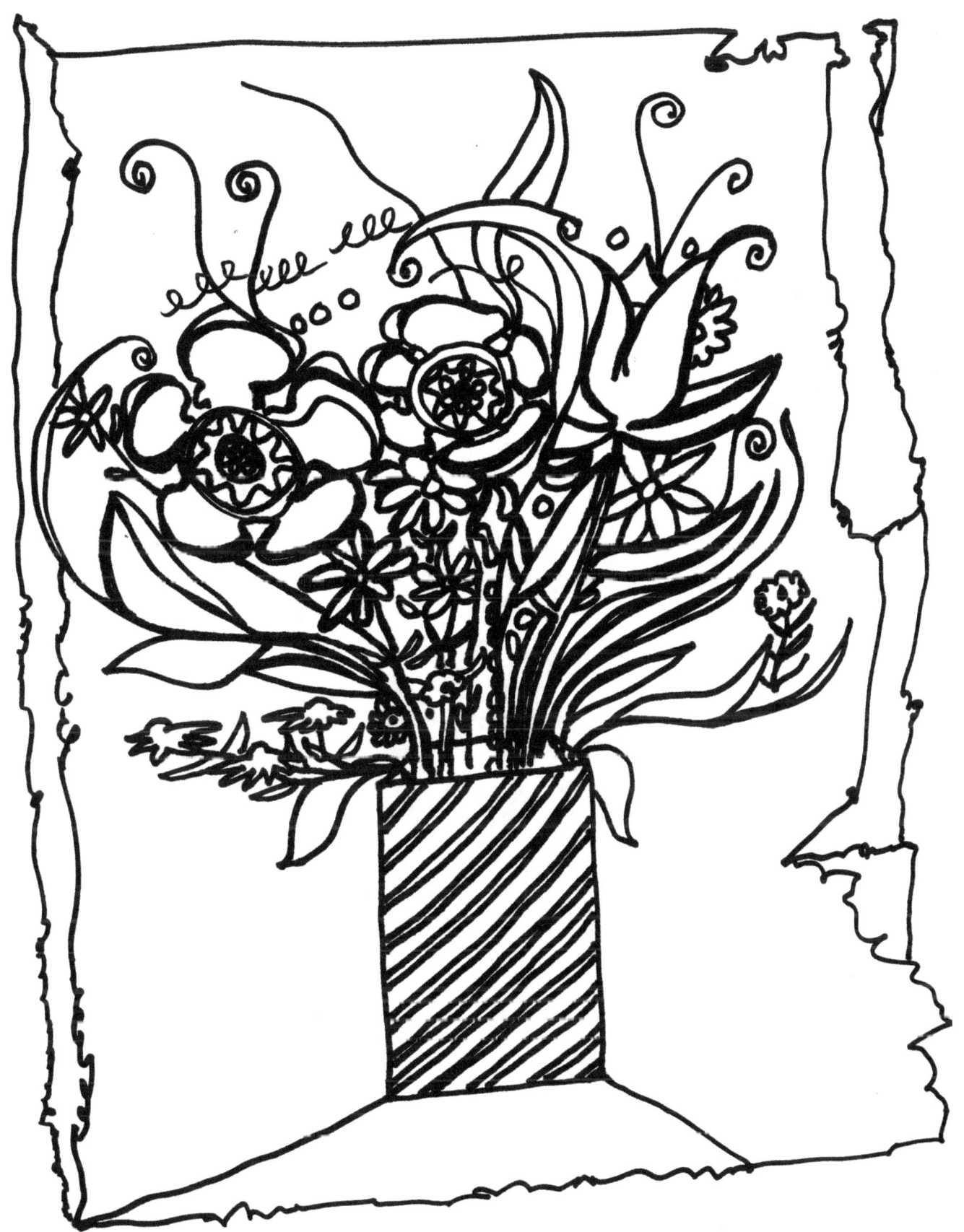

ENCHANTED FLORALS

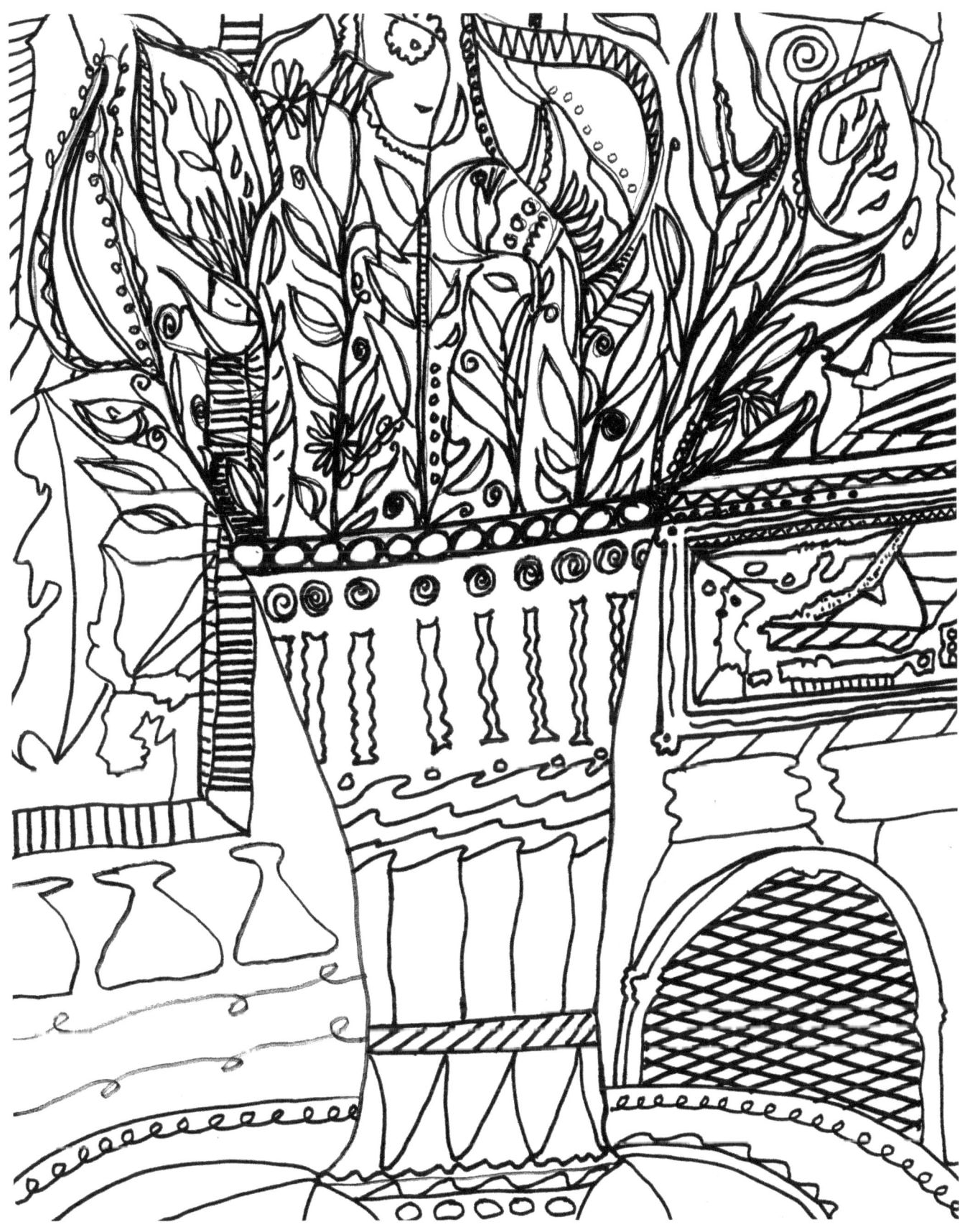

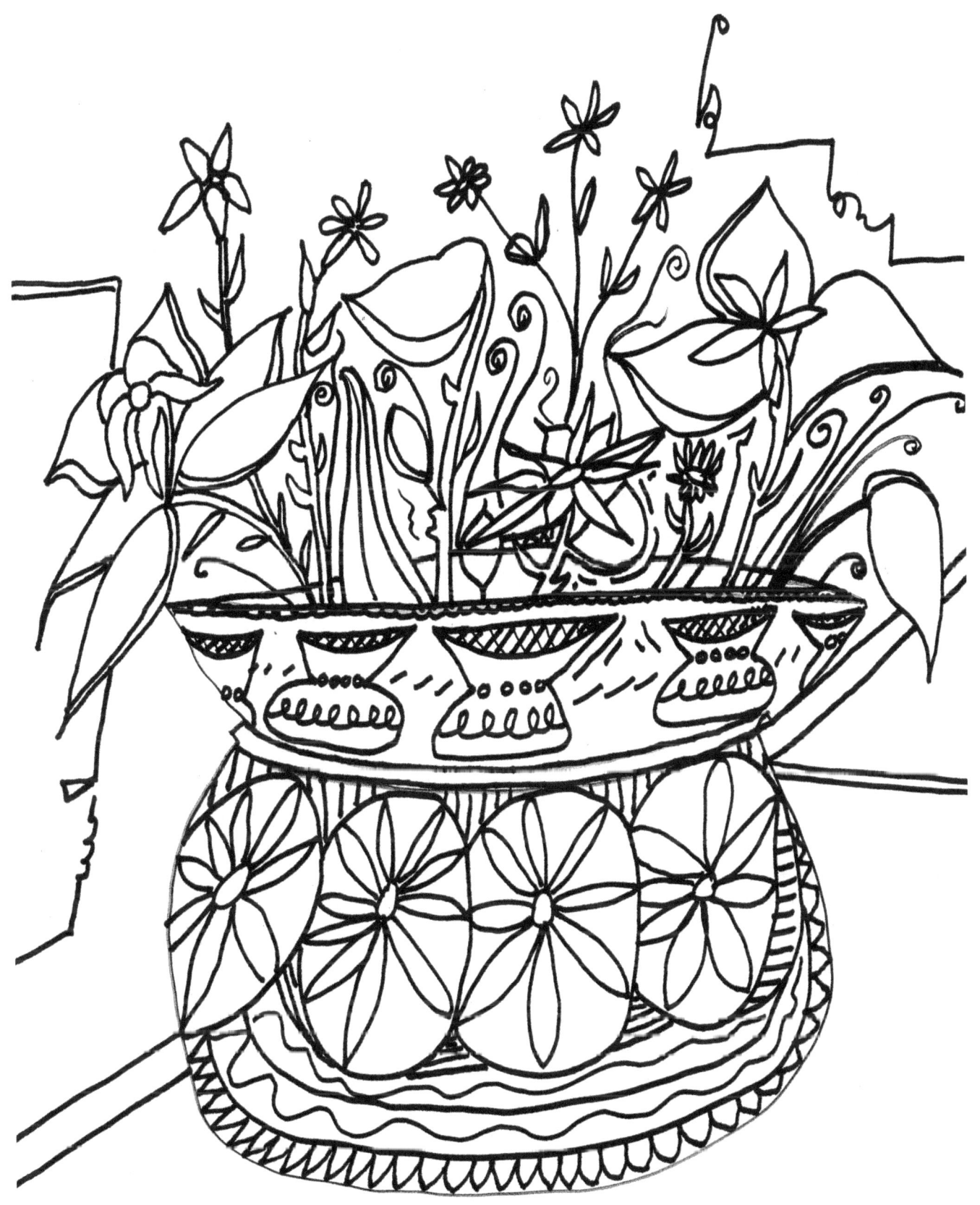

ENCHANTED FLORALS

ENCHANTED FLORALS

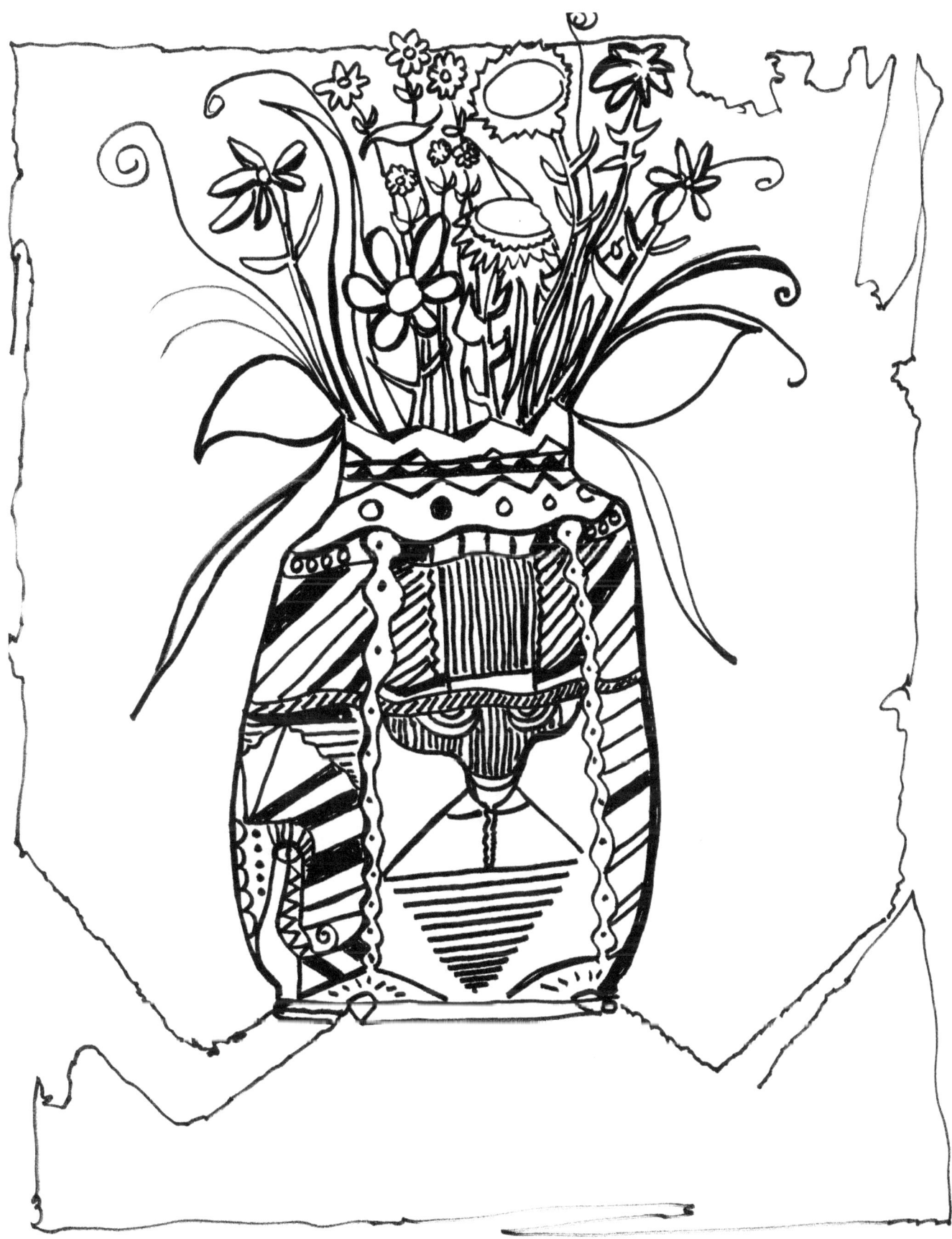

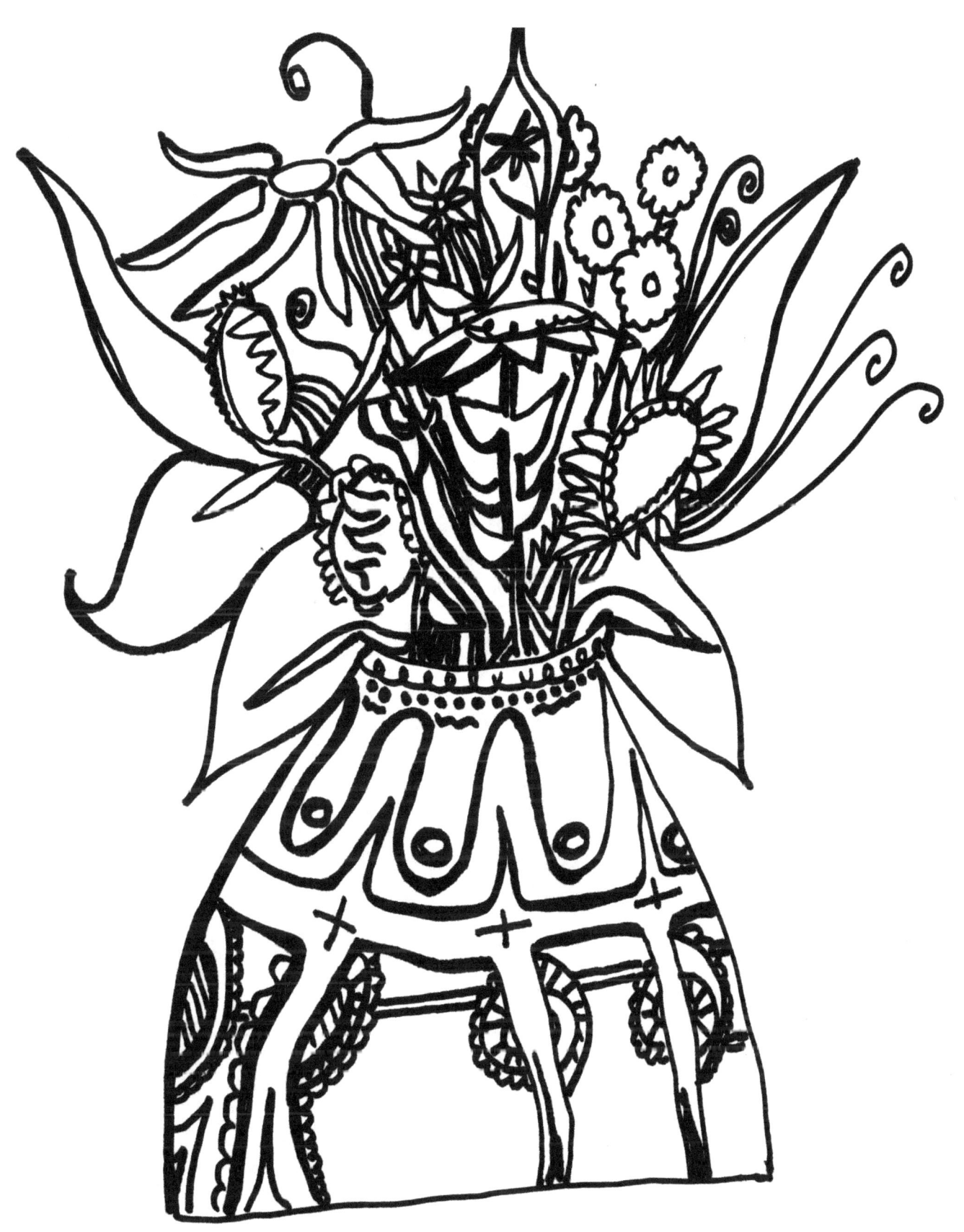

ENCHANTED FLORALS

ENCHANTED FLORALS

ENCHANTED FLORALS

ENCHANTED FLORALS

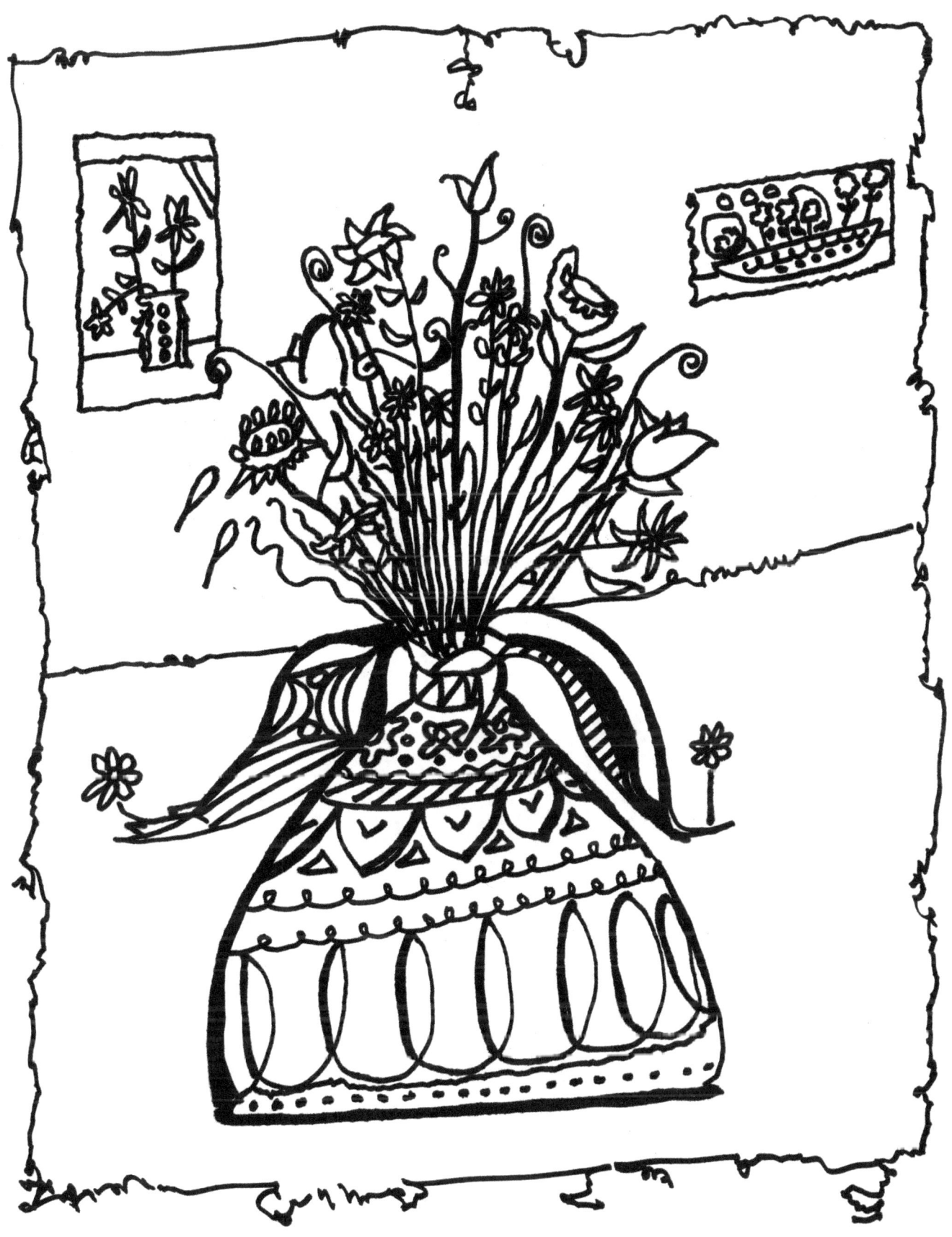

ENCHANTED FLORALS

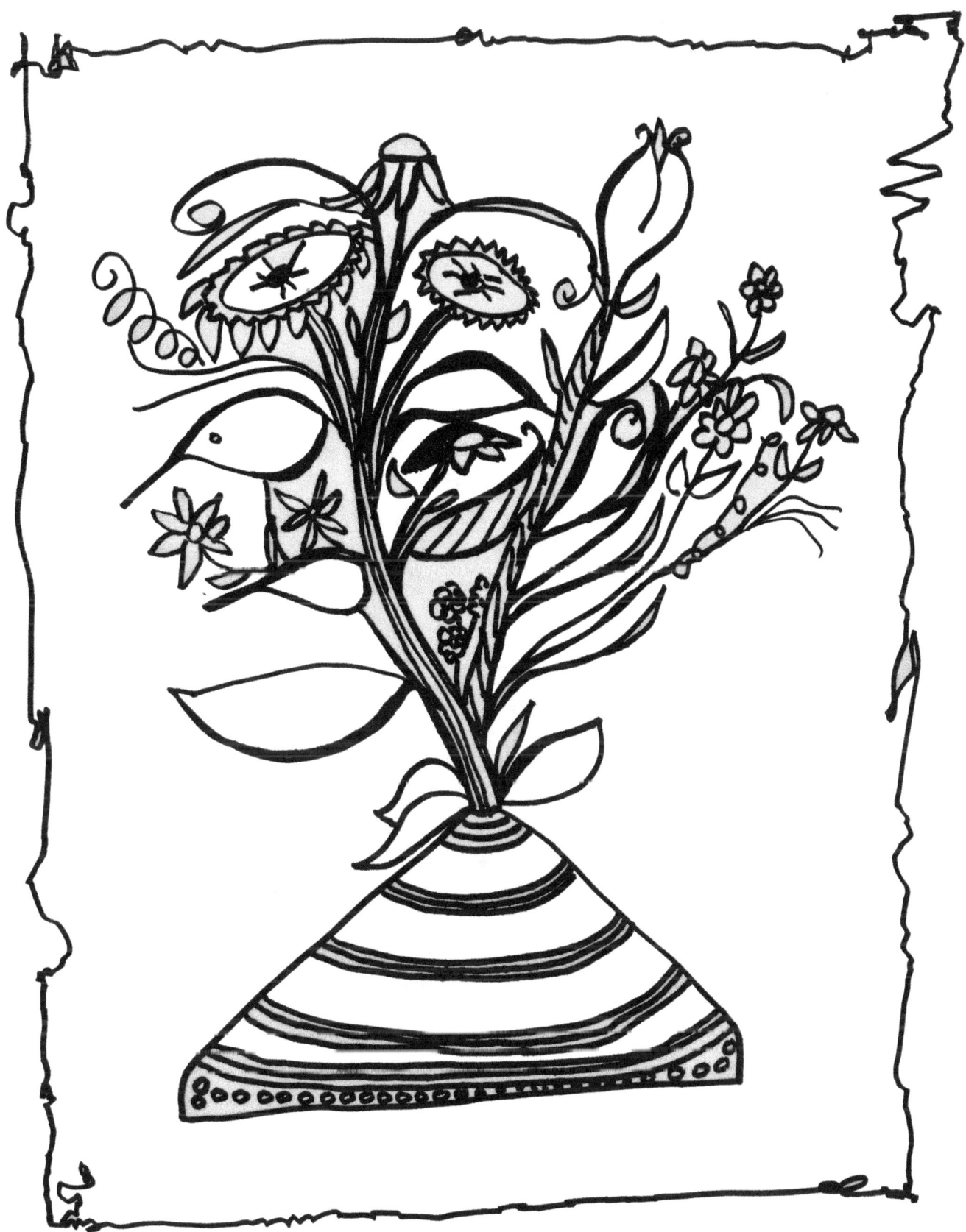

ENCHANTED FLORALS

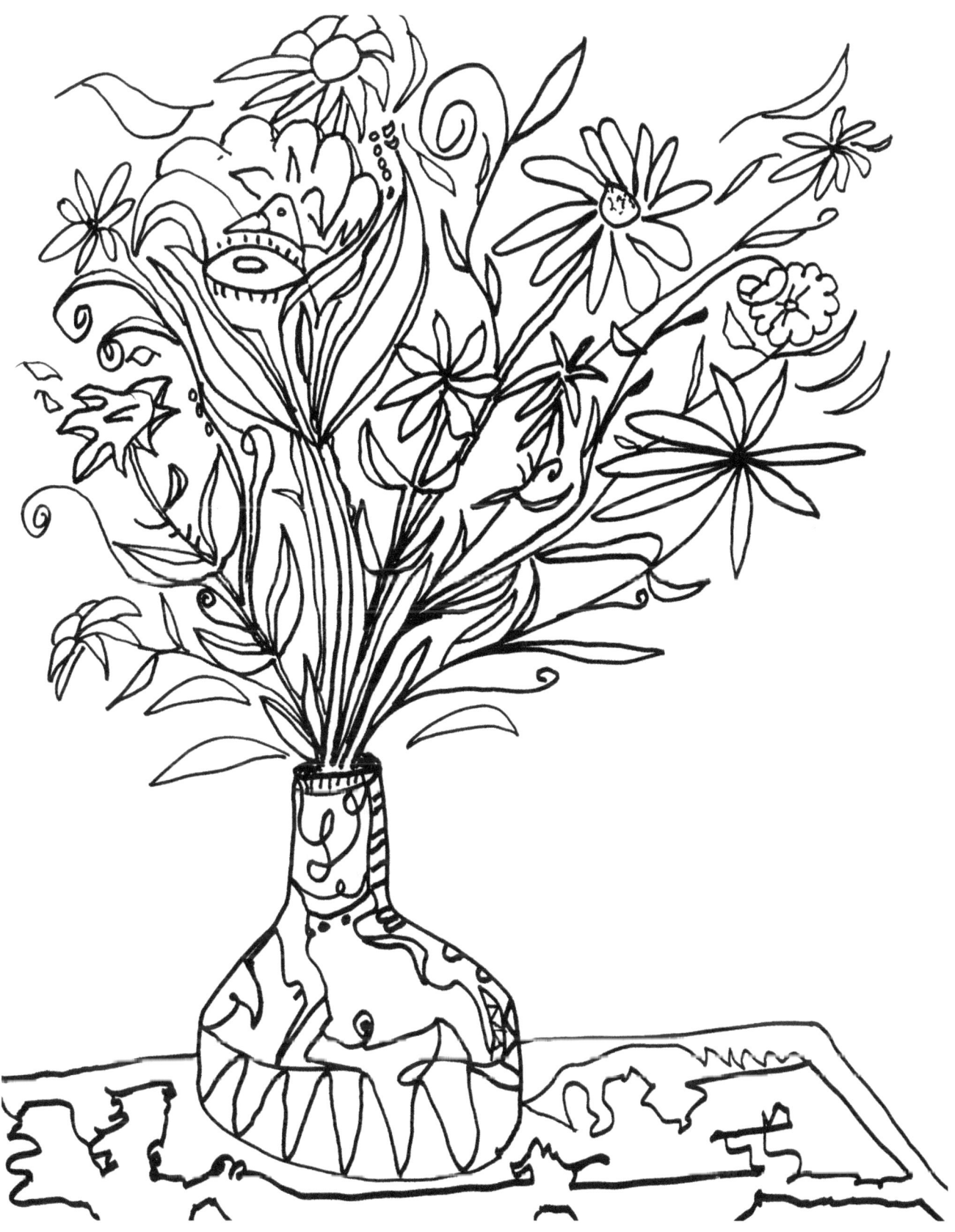

ENCHANTED FLORALS

ENCHANTED FLORALS

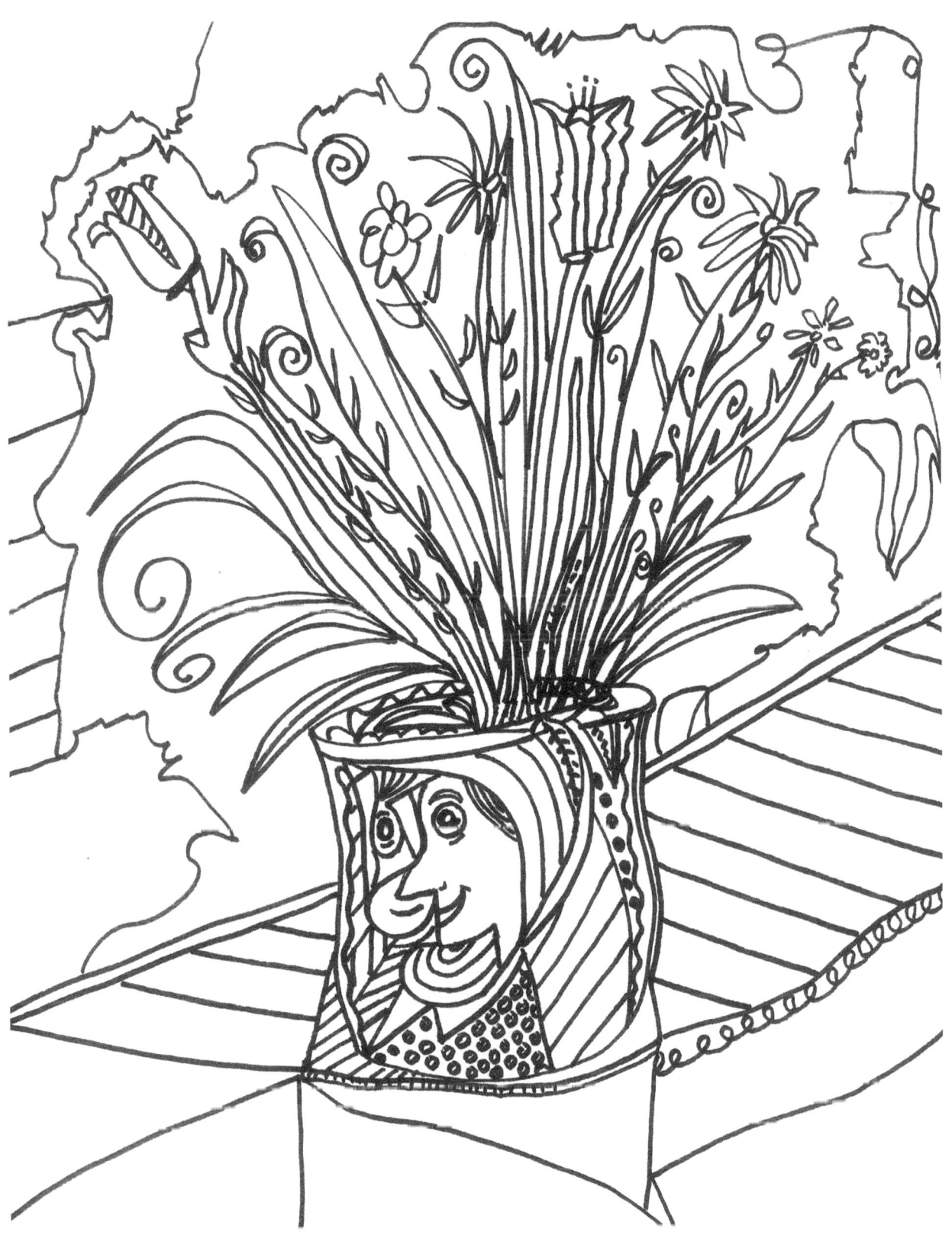

ENCHANTED FLORALS

Create your own Lines

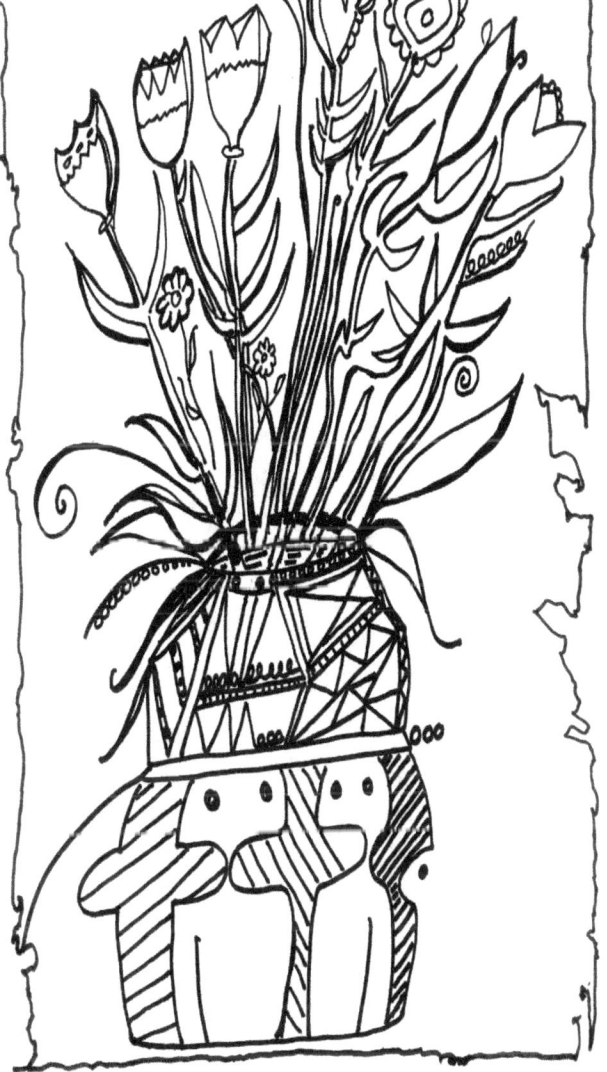

Relax

Frame and Display

Have Fun

Color Outside The Lines

Color Therapy

STEVE STEIN

Steve Stein has been an artist "almost from birth", An extraordinary statement from an extraordinary man. Born in Chicago in 1935 Steve was rarely seen without a crayon in hand gifted to him from his beloved Aunt Adelle. A Self proclaimed "man of many hats" Steve practiced commercial art for several years before opening the Steve Stein Gallery in 1963, in Southern California. While raising his family and making a success of his gallery, Steve never forgot who he always was, an artist of cheerful proportions. His own art is a reflection of his whimsical journey into feeling good about life. It is a story told in color and light that leaves you feeling strangely hopeful about humanity. His primary mediums are acrylics, felt pen and oil pastels on paper and canvas. He also uses parts and pieces from his discarded work, and in doing so creates beautiful compositions and collages.

Of his work Stein says…"I am fulfilled when I paint in my own primitive, impressionistic style. Either consciously or unconsciously I am expressing all the happy and humorous events that I see around me."

Julian Lennon,
"When you buy something from an artist you're buying more than an object. You're buying hundreds of hours of errors and experimentation. You're buying years of frustration and moments of pure joy. You're not buying just one thing, you are buying a piece of a heart, a piece of a soul… a small piece of someone else's life."

Having been a prolific artist over the last six decades has given many art lovers the opportunity to enjoy his works. Steve Stein's pieces can be seen in the homes of film luminaries, music celebrities and on the walls of forward thinking corporate boardrooms.

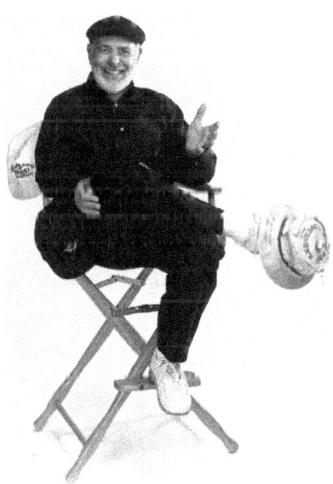